PIRATE RADIO
An Illustrated History

Keith Skues & David Kindred

AMBERLEY

The radio ship *Mi Amigo* was home to several radio stations from 1959 until she sank in the North Sea in March 1980. This photograph was taken in 1975, as the crew of Radio Caroline came on deck to greet visitors.

This edition published 2016
First published 2014

Amberley Publishing
The Hill, Stroud, Gloucestershire, GL5 4EP
www.amberley-books.com

The right of Keith Skues & David Kindred to be identified as the Authors of this work has been asserted in accordance with the Copyrights, Designs and Patents Act 1988.

ISBN 978 1 4456 5905 3 (paperback)
ISBN 978 1 4456 3776 1 (ebook)

British Library Cataloguing in Publication Data.
A catalogue record for this book is available from the British Library.

Typesetting by Amberley Publishing.
Printed in Great Britain.

CONTENTS

Tune

Volume

	Preface	4
	Foreword	6
	Introduction	8
Chapter 1	The Sixties	11
Chapter 2	The Seventies	69
Chapter 3	The Eighties	81
Chapter 4	The Nineties and Noughties	103
Chapter 5	The Ships	110
Chapter 6	The Legend Still Lives On	134
Chapter 7	The Legacy of Offshore Radio	140
	Acknowledgements	151
	Bibliography	152
	Index	154
	About the Authors	160

PREFACE

To Ronan O'Rahilly, the charismatic and enigmatic Irishman who challenged and changed British radio.

Sent to London to pursue a film career, Ronan O'Rahilly veered toward music and worked with Giorgio Gomelski, helping to promote the Rolling Stones and Georgie Fame. It is well known that after being snubbed by the BBC and Radio Luxembourg, as he tried and failed to make them play some music he was promoting, he realised the only solution, and the only way to topple the BBC/Luxembourg monopoly, was to have his own radio station. The result was Caroline – it would change the social and musical climate of Britain forever.

Radio Caroline set Ronan on a collision course with Prime Minister Harold Wilson, who brought in the law intended to suppress the station. This law had the designated effect for a while, but Ronan exacted his revenge in 1970 with some outrageous political campaigning that may well have caused Wilson to lose the general election.

Often, to maintain his veil of secrecy, Ronan did not answer to his own name, calling himself Bobby Kennedy. He admitted to no telephone number, though clearly he had a phone, communicating via telephone boxes or borrowing the phones of shops on London's Kings Road. In the same way, he admitted to no address. While it was an open secret that he lived in a smart square off of the Kings Road, few were ever allowed to go there and the front door was never answered. His obsession with secrecy maybe got out of control, talking in code words and going silent whenever someone passed by, in case they were from the authorities, or 'The Blue Meanies', as he put it. Or, as he joked, 'just because I'm paranoid, that does not mean they are not out to get me.'

Living by his wits and using his considerable powers of persuasion, he maintained Caroline through the seventies and eighties, but was delightfully naïve in terms of engineering, machinery and practical matters. Erecting a mast 300 feet high on *Ross Revenge* was a folly that backfired spectacularly, and he could not understand when improved technology and communication, along with international co-operation, meant that Caroline could no longer be a mystery wrapped in an enigma. By 1990, the house of cards came crashing down, causing him such distress that he maybe never quite recovered from.

In 1991, he married, but again kept this a secret for two decades.

He decided to leave his traditional haunts of the Kings Road and the Chelsea Arts Club and moved to Ireland. He now lives peacefully on the Irish Sea coast in a small village close to Greenore, the family owned port where Caroline was prepared for sea over fifty years ago.

Peter Moore
Radio Caroline
www.radiocaroline.co.uk
July 2014

Right: The MV *Caroline* off Felixstowe, Suffolk, in March 1964. The ship was formerly the Baltic ferry *Fredericia*.

Tune

FOREWORD

Volume

The careers of Keith Skues and myself have been closely intertwined for nearly fifty years. When I was a slip of a lad, I started my broadcasting adventure on an RAF Radio Station in Aden. Some years later, who should appear on the same airwaves but a young 'Cardboard Shoes', aka Keith Skues.

From Aden, I went to Nairobi, Kenya, and so did Keith, where he was a rising star on the British Forces Network. I returned to the UK to join the BBC, where I worked on the popular 'Saturday Club'. In 1967, I started at Radio 1 by producing the first ever programme, the 'Tony Blackburn Breakfast Show'. This new BBC Network was heavily influenced by the recently closed down pirate radio stations. Even there our paths crossed as in preparation for the launch of Radio 1, I had made a clandestine visit to the biggest pirate station, 'Big L' (Radio London), where I was greeted warmly by many of their DJs, among them Keith Skues. Following the closure of 'Big L', Keith came ashore, along

with many of his colleagues, and took up a BBC job as the front man on the very popular 'Saturday Club'. From there, our paths were closely woven together on the radio network. I started 'Radio 1 Club', followed by the 'Radio 1 Roadshow', where Keith proved as popular as ever. So it continued for many years, until the advent of Independent Local Radio, when Keith moved to Sheffield and the fun of Radio Hallam. Even there our paths crossed, as my son, now an eminent professor, was based in Sheffield Hallam University. Even now, as our respective careers are winding down, we meet up regularly in southern Spain, where we reminisce over paella and a glass or three of Rioja.

So what, you may ask, has all this to do with a book on the history of pirate radio? Simply this, Keith and I lived through the sixties, probably the most exciting times in UK broadcasting since it started in 1922. We were lucky enough to experience the growth of young audiences who loved the medium, when up-and-coming DJs were not hamstrung by formats and playlists and could develop as real entertaining personalities. What they put between the records was as entertaining as the records they introduced, and their styles formed the mould for popular music radio as it is today. That is the legacy of the pirates, and no one knows the story of those years better than Keith. A good writer, with many books to his credit, he has brought it all alive for the reader. Good job, too, because before long most of the participants will have forgotten, or passed on to that heavenly wavelength beyond the stars.

Coupled with Keith's expertise and knowledge are the wonderful photographs of Ipswich-born Dave Kindred, who has worked in professional photography for over fifty years. For most of his career, he was a staff photographer with the *East Anglian Daily Times* and *Evening Star*, based in Ipswich. He ended his career with the Archant newspaper group, as picture editor of the *Evening Star*, in January 2004.

He was just seventeen-years-old when Radio Caroline began broadcasting off Felixstowe, Suffolk, in March 1964, providing just the kind of radio teenagers dreamed of. He was always keen to visit the radio ships on his days off, and was lucky to have a pilot friend who would take him off the coast to photograph the ships from the air.

David's photographs of radio ships have been used by publishers over the past fifty years, but they have never been published together, and most have never been used in print before. He is the author, or joint author, of twenty books of images from his collection of vintage photographs.

So you have at your fingertips a complete picture of what we enjoyed all those years ago.

It was a magical time, and one that all fans of popular music lived for and enjoyed as they sampled their music off their newfangled 'trannies'. I hope you are as captivated by the tale as I was and, having read it, you will understand what it was like and share the magic of those pirate airwaves.

Johnny Beerling
Controller BBC Radio 1, 1985–1993
Estepona, Spain
July 2014

Ronan O'Rahilly.

INTRODUCTION

Tune

Volume

Hundreds of men slept in her beds, some of them famous household names. In the 1960s, she was discussed at length in the House of Commons, forcing a change of the law. Some believe her actions altered the result of the 1970 general election.

At times of distress, men have risked their lives to save her homes from ruin. Volunteers still work for her, painting her rusting former home, treating it like a national treasure. Now the naughty, young revolutionary of the 1960s has celebrated her fiftieth birthday in her new home in Kent, with a team of unpaid men and women tending to her every need. Caroline was born 28 March 1964.

Radio Caroline started broadcasting from a ship off the coast of Felixstowe, Suffolk, at Easter, triggering a change in British broadcasting. We still see the effects today. The offshore radio revolution was part of the huge changes in youth culture taking place in the 1960s. The BBC had failed to offer a service to the young listeners who, every day, wanted to hear The Beatles, Rolling Stones, Kinks and The Animals, and other new young bands releasing records. Teenagers loved the new tiny portable radios made possible by transistors, but there was no radio station playing 'pop'.

David Kindred, whose impressive collection of photographs from the offshore radio era form the purpose of this illustrated book, was seventeen when Caroline came on the air, and was excited to find a radio station playing music all day. He had started working for the local newspapers in Ipswich, Suffolk, a year earlier as a trainee photographer. David was the only youngster among a group of older photographers who were not as interested as him in music radio.

One of the most controversial events of the 1960s was the birth of offshore or, as it was later to become known, 'pirate' radio. For listeners, it was the realisation that these stations were providing a service, for the very first time, that made music available any time of day or night. They were operated by young people who were doing their own thing and fighting against the forces of the Establishment. From the freedom of international waters, the pirate radio stations changed the face, and indeed the shape, of British broadcasting.

I was a disc jockey on Radio Caroline South from the summer of 1964 to the end of 1965, and then transferred to Radio London ('Big L') from 1966 to 1967, when we were outlawed by the British Government. Offshore radio was replaced by BBC Radio 1, where a small number of former pirate DJs were employed to work on the national network that began broadcasting on 30 September 1967. I was fortunate to be one of those presenters.

The era of the 1960s was, in my humble opinion, a good time to have been involved in the world of entertainment. Fashion and pop music were leading the way. We had the Mary Quant phenomenon, Carnaby Street, John Stephen 'boutiques', The Beatles and Rolling Stones, top fashion model Jean 'The Shrimp' Shrimpton, photographer David Bailey and flower power, not forgetting offshore radio.

David Kindred made visits to Radio Caroline South when it was anchored off the Essex coast, opposite Walton-on-the-Naze. He soon struck up a friendship with the DJs, most of whom were in their early twenties. Quite often, I would bump into David when attending different functions in Ipswich when on shore leave.

It was in December 1964 that David Kindred saw the MV *Galaxy* for the first time; it had just arrived and was not yet on the air. It was to be home to Radio London for almost three years.

The trips on the tender from Harwich or Felixstowe took about an hour and a half to reach the floating radio stations. The Dutch crew would supply the ships with water, fuel, mail etc., and return to port. This would allow visitors about half an hour on board. David wanted more time to plan and take photographs, so he arranged a couple of trips with an 'overnight'. This gave him more of a chance to capture life on board. He says it was time-consuming to make the journey, so he would use his days off to make the trips.

As the months and years went by, he made a lot of contacts with people in the world of 'watery wireless', who would tip him off about pirate radio stories. He was at Holland-on-Sea, Essex, soon after the *Mi Amigo* ran aground in 1966. He flew over the Radio Northsea International ship in 1970 as it sailed for the English coast, was one of the first to find the mast of the *Mi Amigo* sticking out of the sea in 1980, and the first news photographer on board the *Ross Revenge* in 1983. The stories had to be connected to Suffolk and Essex to be of interest to his newspapers, although he was often as near to Kent as he was to Essex!

All the photographs in the book were taken by David Kindred, except where credited. Now, fifty years since the birth of Radio Caroline, David still has fond memories of yesteryear:

Rolling around the North Sea, sometimes in small boats, to then leap on board the radio ship or flying low over the waves was always great fun and I would not have missed those days for anything.

Radio broadcasting from ships on the high seas, or on rusty Second World War forts in the Thames Estuary, only existed for three-and-a-half years, until it was made illegal. It is amazing that, fifty years later, thousands of listeners still have happy memories of the days of 'watery wireless'.

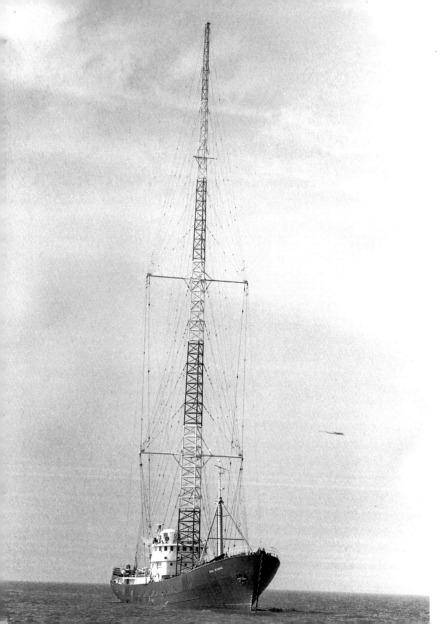

Pirate radio did carry on illegally after the Marine Etc., Broadcasting (Offences) Bill became an Act of Parliament. Photographs of these ships, and some of their broadcasters, are included in this book.

Varying amounts of literature has been published about the offshore radio days, including a book I wrote in 1994 (reprinted 2009) *Pop Went the Pirates*.

I have kept in touch with David Kindred over the past fifty years, and many of his non-pirate radio photographs appear in numerous books about life in Suffolk and East Anglia. However, never before has a book been published devoted to an illustrated history of pirate radio. David did not visit every ship or fort off the British coastline, but mention is made of all the stations in the text.

Enjoy your travels in the wonderful world of watery wireless.

Keith Skues
Norfolk, 2014

Left: The Radio Caroline ship, *Ross Revenge*, with its spectacular 300-foot mast in 1983.

Chapter 1
THE SIXTIES

Radio Caroline began transmissions from a ship off the coast of Felixstowe, Suffolk, at Easter 1964 – it would start a radio revolution among young people.

The BBC had failed to offer a service to the young listeners who wanted to hear the popular songs of that era – The Beatles, Rolling Stones, Kinks, The Animals and other new young bands releasing records. Their programmes were made up of the Home Service, mainly a talk station, the Radio 4 of its time. The Light Programme was a mix of entertainment, including a live lunchtime variety show like 'Workers Playtime', comedy shows 'Hancock's Half Hour' and 'Round the Horne', and a radio soap, 'Mrs Dale's Diary'.

Most popular music programmes would include a BBC orchestra playing the latest tunes. I was a great fan of the BBC Northern Dance Orchestra (NDO), based in Manchester. However, with great respect, teenagers did not want the NDO to play The Beatles and the Stones music. In their defence, BBC programme producers were tied by a limit on the amount of commercial gramophone records' 'needle time' that could be broadcast. An agreement with the Musicians' Union meant that relatively few record programmes were heard. The most popular show on radio at that time was 'Two Way Family Favourites', broadcast on a Sunday lunchtime and devoted exclusively to record requests, as a consequence its audience was huge. Other popular request programmes were 'Housewives' Choice' and 'Childrens' Favourites'. Two programmes that attracted teenagers at weekends were the 'Saturday Club', once described as 'a two-hour experimental teenage show', and 'Easy Beat', both of which comprised records and live music. 'Pick of the Pops' also enjoyed a sizeable audience.

Unlike today, where there are hundreds of disc jockeys and radio presenters making a living, only a handful existed on the BBC in

The *Mi Amigo* arrived off the Essex coast, 27 April 1964, to broadcast Radio Atlanta. Radios Caroline and Atlanta merged in July 1964, and the MV *Caroline* sailed to Ramsey Bay off the Isle of Man to become Radio Caroline North.

the early to mid-1960s, including David Jacobs, Brian Matthew, Pete Murray, Alan Freeman, Keith Fordyce, Don Moss, Franklin Engelmann and Derek McCullock, known as 'Uncle Mac'.

By 1964, technology had moved on and we were buying transistor radios (known as the 'tranny'). For the first time in our lives, radio had become portable. The large, electrically heated valve sets that our parents owned were not on our shopping list. Transistor radios were the way forward, and we could enjoy pop music all day and night thanks to the offshore radio stations. Music was important to teenagers. The words of songs expressed our feelings as we came to terms with ourselves. Parents could not understand us. Neither could our teachers at school. The pirate stations managed to reach out to teenagers and young housewives in a language all could understand.

With no commercial or local broadcasting in the United Kingdom, the only continuous pop music radio was from the distant Radio Luxembourg, which broadcast music shows sponsored by record companies to Britain in the evenings. Their signal faded badly, and the sponsored programmes played only parts of tracks to promote sales. You might have heard just a minute of a current single with announcers talking over much of the track.

Radio Ships Broadcasting from International Waters

Twenty-three-year-old Irishman Ronan O'Rahilly picked up on an idea, which had worked off the coasts of Holland and Scandinavia, to fit a ship as a radio station that could operate outside the British territorial limit of 3 miles.

In January 1964, by chance, O'Rahilly met Allan Crawford, a music publisher who had completed plans to launch Britain's first offshore commercial radio station – Radio Atlanta. Crawford took O'Rahilly into his confidence, thinking he had a prospective backer. Big mistake! He was in for a shock two months later. O'Rahilly told Crawford that his father owned the Port of Greenore in southern Ireland, and the location was an ideal place to fit out a pirate radio ship. Both men firmly believe they were the first with the idea of broadcasting offshore. However, as early as 1934, broadcasts were taking place off the British coast, but none survived for any length of time.

Broadcasting pop music from a ship became popular in 1958, with Radio Mercur broadcasting from international waters off the Danish coast. The station transmitted from the ship *Cheeta* and, later in 1962, from the *Lucky Star*. But luck ran out in 1962 when armed Danish police with customs men escorted the ship *Lucky Star* into port. The Danish government had brought a court injunction against the radio station and it was closed down.

Offshore radio began in Holland in 1960, when Radio Veronica commenced broadcasting in Dutch from the MV *Borkum Riff* off Scheveningen. English programmes were first transmitted on 16 February 1961 on 192 metres. They broadcast under the call sign CNBC (Commercial Neutral Broadcasting Company). The disc jockeys were Doug Stanley, Paul Hollingdale, John Michael and Bob Fletcher. All programmes were pre-recorded in London and Hilversum. There were no English personnel on the ship.

It was also in 1961 that Radio Nord began broadcasting from the Panamanian registered ship *Magda Maria*. Transmissions to Sweden began on 8 March, but she suffered damage in a storm in December 1961 and was put into Sandhamn for repairs. Radio Nord ceased broadcasting on 30 June 1962.

In 1962, Arnold Swanson began preparing a station to be called GBOK, broadcasting on 388 metres from the Nore in the Thames Estuary. However, the project failed as Swanson, who already had a ship, ran into financial trouble.

Mrs Britt Wadner, a forty-seven-year-old Swedish grandmother, bought a ship and began broadcasting to Sweden on 1 April 1962, calling her station Radio Syd. She was eventually arrested and, in 1964, jailed. Ten thousand Swedish Radio Syd fans then gatecrashed Hinsberg Prison, where she was serving a three-month sentence. She was released after serving just four weeks.

Back in London, Allan Crawford had been making good progress in finding backers for Project Atlanta. However, with the news of Britt Wadner being jailed for illegally broadcasting pop music, potential backers lost interest and walked away.

Ronan O'Rahilly was steaming ahead with his plans. In a television interview I did with him in 1977, he told me that he set up Radio Caroline because he did not mind that it was illegal or criminal in any way: 'I guess there was a whole bunch of us at the time who, I think, were pretty wild, young and rebellious. I believe it was the beginning of a revolution and a better world for it.'

So why the name Caroline? Ronan says the biggest influence on him at the time was John F. Kennedy. When he became president in 1960, he raised the expectations of the American population and wanted people to do things themselves:

The actual moment of decision to call the station Radio Caroline was when I was flying across the Atlantic and I opened up the *Life* magazine. Right across the centre spread was a photograph of President Kennedy in his Oval Office and, climbing under his desk, disrupting the whole work of government, was his daughter Caroline and she was smiling. That kind of imagery very much turned me on and that is when I said the station would be called 'Caroline'.

Years later, researchers proved that the young person climbing under his desk was in fact the President's son, John F. Kennedy Jnr, not Caroline. But why let the truth get in the way of a good story!

As to the Easter launch, Ronan O'Rahilly remembered that it was Easter time when his grandfather, one of the leaders of the Easter uprising in Dublin, was shot by the English when storming a British machine-gun post, outside the post office in 1916. Ronan stated, 'It would appear that I was taking an Easter revenge against English authorities. I guess I was!'

Radio Caroline began test transmissions on Good Friday, 1964. Regular programmes began at noon the following day. Broadcaster Simon Dee announced, 'This is Radio Caroline on 199, your all-day music station. We are on the air every day from six in the morning till six at night. The time right now is one minute past twelve and that means it's time for Christopher Moore.'

This was a pre-recorded programme, where Moore wished listeners a Happy Easter and thanked all the people who had worked hard to put the station on-air, particularly Ronan O'Rahilly. The first track he played was 'Not Fade Away' by the Rolling Stones.

The first live broadcast from Radio Caroline was presented by Simon Dee. The station's management and backers were not sure if the Royal Navy would be called to tow them away, or if anybody was listening. Within days, sacks of mail from listeners

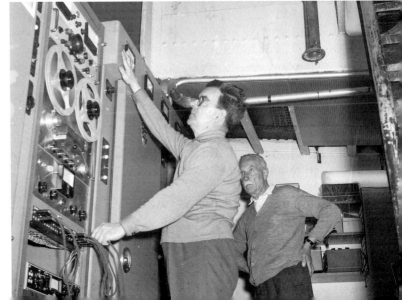

Above: Chef Leendert Noort preparing a meal in the galley of the *Mi Amigo* for the staff of Radio Atlanta in May 1964. With him is Irene Meijer, the wife of the ship's skipper.

Above right: Members of the ships' crew in the mess room of the *Mi Amigo* in May 1964.

Right: The transmitter hold on the *Mi Amigo* during the Radio Atlanta days in the spring of 1964.

Left: Radio Atlanta's station manager Richard Harris in the broadcast studio on the *Mi Amigo* in May 1964. The studio then even had fancy curtains (*top left*)!

arrived on board. The station was an instant hit with listeners – the sheer cheek of it was part of the appeal.

Although young presenters with a relaxed style staffed the station, its music format in the early days stuck to a very British format. There was music for housewives and workers in the morning, pop music at lunchtime and music from films and shows in the afternoons. We then heard more Top 20 tracks for students returning from school and college late afternoon, followed by a request show.

On Easter Sunday 1964, many yachts, motor boats, catamarans and light aircraft arrived at Felixstowe to view the radio ship that was flying the Jolly Roger flag. Journalists and photographers joined the onlookers. Commercial radio had arrived in Britain and the national press gave it wide acclaim.

A Gallup Opinion Poll took place, and we learned that nearly 7 million listeners tuned into Radio Caroline on 199 metres in the first three weeks. Children under the age of seventeen were not interviewed.

Radio Atlanta Arrives

Six weeks after Radio Caroline began broadcasting, Radio Atlanta, aboard the *Mi Amigo*, sailed in and anchored some 14 miles from Radio Caroline in international waters, opposite Walton-on-the-Naze, Essex.

Radio Atlanta had hoped to be on-air before Radio Caroline. Allan Crawford, determined to launch offshore radio to a British audience, had been working out details for close on four years. Radio Nord, which would become MV *Mi Amigo*, had

been broadcasting to Sweden from the Baltic Sea, but when the Swedish government introduced legislation against pirate ships, Radio Nord was closed down. Crawford and his directors purchased the Radio Nord ship, and test transmissions began off the Essex coast on 9 May 1964. Regular programmes began on 12 May, with Australian DJ Colin Nichol presenting the first scheduled programme – 'The Breakfast Show'.

Caroline and Atlanta Merger

On 2 July 1964, Radios Caroline and Atlanta merged operations. They announced that in future they would broadcast under the one call sign, Caroline, but from two different locations. MV *Caroline* would sail to the Isle of Man, a self-governing British Crown dependency, on 3 July 1964, and anchor at a position 5 miles off Ramsey, broadcasting on 199 metres. The radio signal would be heard in the north of England, the Midlands, Ireland, Scotland and Wales.

MV *Mi Amigo* would remain in its present position off the Essex coast, and broadcast to the London area and South East England under the Radio Caroline call sign, also on 199 metres. It would also be heard in Holland, France, Belgium, Norway, Sweden and Finland.

The Caroline-Atlanta merger represented a floating investment of £500,000. The main reason for the amalgamation of Radios Atlanta and Caroline made business sense, so as to not compete for the limited amount of advertising that was available at that time.

Sir Jocelyn Stevens, former owner of the British high society magazine *Queen*, and later chairman of English Heritage, was a major shareholder of Radio Caroline. In April 1964, he told *The Times*, 'One doesn't take the whole thing too seriously, and one recognises the skull and crossbones. We really do get on very well together. It did not need so much as a blind eye to see the possibilities of a merger.'

The new team of disc jockeys for Radio Caroline South was Simon Dee, Doug Kerr, Keith Martin, Tony Withers, Peter Du Crow and Bryan Vaughan.

The MV *Caroline*, under the command of Captain Hengeveld, sailed from Felixstowe and arrived in Ramsey Bay on 6 July 1964. The ship had been broadcasting non-stop pop music as she sailed west around the England and Wales coast. The DJs on board were Tom Lodge, Jerry Leighton and Alan 'Neddy' Turner.

Tom Lodge had been a London reporter for the CBC, the Canadian state broadcaster, and had met Ronan O'Rahilly in a pub in the Kings Road, Chelsea. He was so interested in Ronan's plans had that he quit his reporting job and joined Caroline shortly after its first broadcasts. Jerry Leighton had been a fashion designer, singer, compère, comedian and script writer before he joined Radio Caroline. Alan Turner followed the short careers of policeman, salesman and engineer before joining the MV *Fredericia* as a radio engineer, but soon transferred to become an on-air presenter. Along with Tom and Jerry, he broadcast radio shows while the ship sailed round the English coast and Wales, before arriving off the Isle of Man.

Alan, who now operates an aviation maintenance facility in Kent, still remembers that epic journey fifty years ago:

We set sail at midnight on Friday 3 July 1964. The next morning Tom Lodge rushed into my cabin and said have a look through the porthole. We were off the Sussex coast and Beachy Head was packed with dozens of visitors. I thought it would be a good idea to acknowledge them and decided to unscrew the large mirror over my wash basin in my cabin and took it on deck. It was a sunny day and I began flashing the shoreline. The response was magical. Thousands of mirrors and car headlights returned the flashing. This continued all the way along the south coast, so on Saturday 4 July the famous Caroline flashing was born.

A speedboat came out to see us off Land's End and the owner threw a selection of newspapers on board.

We eventually arrived at the Isle of Man in the afternoon of Monday 6 July 1964 – Tynwald Day, the Isle of Man's celebration of the world's oldest Parliament. It was an amazing journey and one I will never forget.

In August 1965, Radio Caroline received positive feedback from the Isle of Man Tourist Board. The DJs had been giving the island free publicity for several months. The tourist board expressed their wish that Caroline could be brought ashore to carry on their good work. Unfortunately, the mandarins in Whitehall did not go along with the Isle of Man's suggestion.

While the northern ship was enjoying success, there was trouble at sea on the *Mi Amigo*. On 27 July 1964, disc jockey Bryan Vaughan was taken ill with suspected food poisoning. Chief disc jockey Simon Dee asked the captain for permission to have Bryan taken off the ship. The captain refused, accusing him of 'mutiny'. Simon interrupted his programme and broadcast an SOS message appealing to listeners to send a boat out to Radio Caroline as soon as possible.

Simon recalled the incident when we met at a Caroline reunion in London in March 2004: 'The Walton and Frinton lifeboat was launched and, when it drew alongside, the captain accused me of mutiny and told me I was only a disc jockey and nobody goes off the ship unless I say so.'

Bryan Vaughan was eventually taken off the *Mi Amigo* aboard the lifeboat. He was detained in Clacton Hospital for two weeks, and later returned to Radio Caroline to continue broadcasting. Now resident in Sydney, Australia, but meeting the author in Amsterdam, March 2014, Bryan remembers:

At a distance, details become somewhat hazy but, as I recall, I had just finished the morning shift having felt unwell throughout my show. The weather was fine and, in any case, I was rarely affected by sea sickness, so that was no excuse. The exit from the studio led directly into our mess and recreation room. I opened the door and the next thing I remembered was waking up in my cabin downstairs. I had terrible stomach pains and thought that it might be an appendicitis attack. I had experienced a couple of these in previous years.

As I learnt later, Simon Dee had broadcast my plight over the airwaves and the Walton and Frinton lifeboat rushed to my rescue. I was helped upstairs by some of the crew and disc jockeys and eventually taken aboard the lifeboat. As was his right, the captain was very vocal in his protests against me being removed from the *Mi Amigo* but frankly, at that stage, I was beyond argument and pretty much out of it. It was not a particularly

Right: The Radio Caroline ship *Fredericia* from the air in April 1964.

long voyage to the Walton Pier, where I was landed and loaded on a waiting ambulance. I was to spend the best part of ten days at Clacton Hospital, where I was eventually diagnosed with acute food poisoning. I remain forever grateful to the Walton and Frinton lifeboat community and have visited their headquarters on a couple of occasions over the years.

As for Simon Dee? He was ordered off the *Mi Amigo* in disgrace and went to work at Caroline House in Chesterfield Gardens, Mayfair, London. He later joined the BBC and became a popular TV presenter with his twice-weekly show *Dee Time* attracting audiences of 18 million. Simon (real name Cyril Nicholas Henty-Dodd) died of bone cancer on 29 August 2009, at the age of seventy-four.

Government Expresses Concern About the Pirates

Immediately after Christmas, the Postmaster General, Anthony Wedgwood Benn, who succeeded Reginald Bevins in October 1964 following a Labour Party victory at the polls, said that the government was expected to act against the pirates operating from around the British coasts early in 1965.

In a debate in the House of Commons in May 1965, he said,

Whatever future there might be for sound broadcasting in this country, the pirate stations have no part of it. These stations, which started last year, were designed to force the hand of Parliament on the future development of sound radio. That has been made crystal clear many times.

As I have said time and time again in the House, the stealing of copyright, the endangering of the livelihood of musicians, the appropriation of wavelengths, the interference with foreign stations, the danger to shipping and ship to shore radio made the pirates a menace.

At that time in history, the pirates were not breaking any laws. Radios Caroline and London were broadcasting in international waters, beyond the 3-mile limit, and outside the jurisdiction of the British Isles.

Journey Out to Radio Caroline South

My first visit to Caroline House was on 2 July 1964, the day of the merger between Caroline and Atlanta. I signed a contract to join the Radio Caroline South ship, but had to wait until 31 August, when I made my way from London to Parkeston Quay, Harwich. I met up with DJs Doug Kerr, Keith Martin and Tony Blackburn to serve my first fortnight aboard a pirate radio ship.

On arrival at Parkeston Quay, we were met by Bill Scadden, a former CID inspector at Scotland Yard. He had served twenty-five years in the police in this country and overseas, and was now the Caroline liaison officer. He supervised us going through HM Customs and Excise, where we had to show our passports as we were officially leaving the country. There were also other checks made with HM Waterguard, HM Immigration, the Special Branch of the CID, together with a dozen other organisations, including the Port of Health Authority and the local Harbour Board.

The tender *Offshore 1* alongside the Radio Caroline South ship *Mi Amigo*.

Eventually, we boarded *Offshore 1*, a scarred diesel tender that was far from comfortable. It was manned by three Dutchmen, and one of them told me it was built for utility rather than for comfort.

We finally pulled alongside the *Mi Amigo*, formerly Radio Atlanta and, prior to that, Radio Nord. I was beginning to think 'what have I let myself in for?' The ship was very rusty and much smaller than I had imagined. However, there was a welcoming party on deck. We still had to negotiate a perilous death-defying leap from *Offshore 1* onto the *Mi Amigo* and into a crowd of eager hands to ensure we did not disappear into the North Sea.

I was introduced to everyone on board, from the captain to the chef. There were four DJs, a panel operator, Dutch and English engineers, and three people who represented the programme planning department and looked after the small record library on board. Four people on this shift were Australian.

The *Mi Amigo* was to be my home for the next sixteen months.

The Queen's Christmas Speech

With the two Caroline ships at sea for their first Christmas, the stations wanted to broadcast the Queen's speech on Christmas Day. The BBC refused Radio Caroline to broadcast the pre-recorded speech because Caroline was not an authorised radio station. A Buckingham Palace spokesman said he believed the Queen's speech was available to any broadcaster, but the BBC made the final decision.

Left: DJs Doug Kerr (*left*) and Simon Dee reading Christmas cards from listeners on the *Mi Amigo* in December 1964.

Life on Board the Ship

I had been a presenter/producer with the British Forces Network in Germany, Kenya and Aden, but this was my first attempt of regular broadcasting to England.

Life on board a pirate radio ship was a combination of isolation, claustrophobia and a kind of deprived hip euphoria. There was a spirit of adventure and challenge that certainly came through in the programmes. Although we were onboard for two weeks at a time, we did succeed in communicating to our audiences with a feeling of fun, excitement and freedom, which the BBC and Radio Luxembourg could not convey.

Radio Caroline South broadcast from a relatively small ship. Registered as the merchant vessel *Mi Amigo* (My Friend), she weighed in at 470 tons, was 150 feet in length, had a beam of 24 feet and was capable of travelling at a speed of 8 knots.

We were anchored 3½ miles off the Essex coastline. We all enjoyed our broadcasting, played the records that appealed to a mass audience and had fun. Our enthusiasm was genuine. According to a National Opinion Poll, there was an audience of some 12 million.

The downside of spending a fortnight on a small ship was no contact with land. In that era, there were no computers, no mobile phones, no Facebook or Twitter and no email facilities. We were literally cut off from the rest of the world. The *Offshore 1* tender brought provisions, memos from headquarters and sacks of mail. As DJs, we lived for correspondence from our listeners, who wrote to us in their thousands. They sent us presents as well – food parcels, cuddly toys, scarves, socks, gloves, woolly hats and sweaters.

The Radio Caroline South ship was commanded by a Dutch captain who had a crew of seven, including a chief engineer. The main studio was cramped. You could have two other people in the studio (standing room only), but that was it – no more room. The studio had two portholes so we could see what was going on out at sea and also view the Essex coastline. Sometimes it was on the left, other times it was on the right. It depended very much on the tides, as the ship wrapped itself around the anchor chains. On one occasion, I was surprised and amused when DJ Bryan Vaughan announced on his morning programme, 'I have just seen a car go past the porthole without a driver at the wheel.' Had we drifted into port? No, it was a car on board a cargo ship travelling from Harwich to Hook of Holland.

The main studio and control room on the *Mi Amigo* was self-contained, with two Gates turntables and two Ampex tape machines. The advertisements or pre-recorded shows were played in from the tape machines. There were three Spotmaster cartridge machines for jingles. Next door was a small studio from where the news was broadcast. No equipment was kept here, just a microphone, a desk and a chair.

When I joined Caroline, a panel operator was used to play records, advertisements and jingles. There was a feeling among the DJs that we should in future be 'self op', thus operating the equipment ourselves. It was confusing at first, and worrying if you opened a wrong fader while talking to your audience. In my case, I was fortunate as I had learned my craft with Forces radio overseas where we were all 'self op.' Nowadays, most DJs and radio presenters operate newer digital equipment themselves.

From the studio, the Radio Caroline programme made its way to the transmitter room through the 10 kilowatt transmitter

Above: The record library of the *Mi Amigo*, with Tom Lodge (*left*) Rosko and Rick Dane reading listeners' mail.

Left: During the summertime in the 1960s, visitors to the radio ships on both organised trips and small private craft were a regular feature. The ships were then just outside the British territorial waters and in clear sight of land.

Right: A member of the Dutch crew preparing a meal on the *Mi Amigo*.

and up to the aerial that consisted of a folded dipole, of which the mast was one leg, and a sausage aerial the other. Caroline North's aerial height was 168 feet above the deck, whereas Caroline South's was 157 feet.

There were three decks on the *Mi Amigo*. The top deck was where two lifeboats were housed. The middle deck was the largest, containing the two studios, the control room, the central mess, the galley, toilet and showers. The Dutch crew were accommodated aft on this deck. The bottom deck housed the transmitter, the sleeping quarters, the stateroom (that was later turned into the record library), the provision store and fridges, and also the captain's quarters.

Disc jockeys shared cabins, normally two per room. Having said that, my accommodation was in the worst possible place on the ship. I spent three tours in the forecastle. My bunk was situated next to the paint store. Apart from a horrendous smell, one had to put up with the ship's constant pitching and rolling, tossing and turning, and the slow, monotonous creaking of the anchor chains. Not an easy place to relax and eventually catch up on sleep. There was talk among the Dutch crew that a Swedish engineer had died here many years previous.

The pay we received as disc jockeys was minimal, but we did not have any expenditure on board. Accommodation, food, drink and cigarettes all came with the job.

The *Mi Amigo* was propelled by a 200 horsepower diesel engine with a single screw. Off the Isle of Man, Caroline North was a much larger ship. She was 763 tons, 188 feet in length and had a beam of 32 feet. The MV *Caroline* could reach 14 knots and was propelled by a 1,000 horsepower diesel engine with a single screw.

The record library was the place where most DJs gathered. There were so many new singles coming on board each week space that was rapidly running out. The captain authorised new shelves to be built in the stateroom to house a collection of some 8,000 records. There were occasions during rough weather that the records and the shelves parted company and crashed to the floor.

As news of Radio Caroline South spread across London and the Home Counties, some listeners travelled to the Essex coast to have a closer look at the ship. Soon it became a business to operate tours aboard the *Lady Kent* from the Albion breakwater at Walton-on-the-Naze, and from Clacton-on-Sea in the *Viking Saga*. No visitors were allowed on board, but we would talk with them from the *Mi Amigo*. It was a highlight of the day to greet the visitors and sign autographs.

One unexpected visitor arrived on 20 April 1965. I was returning with Bryan Vaughan after a week's shore leave. After we were dropped off at the *Mi Amigo*, the tender went to Radio London to take some relief disc jockeys. As she was midway between the two ships, an F-101 Voodoo tactical fighter jet crashed into the North Sea, narrowly missing the tender. It had suffered an engine fire and instrument failure that forced the pilot to bail out. A parachute was seen falling into the sea. The tender went full steam ahead.

The pilot was American First Lieutenant John C. Winn Jr, who had flown from his base in Laon, France. He freed himself from his parachute in the air and dropped into the sea. Cutting off his boots with a knife, he started swimming in the ice cold water. He was picked up by DJs Pete Brady and Dave Dennis, and the tender that took him to Radio London, where he changed into dry clothes.

The tender made an emergency call to Harwich Hospital to have an ambulance waiting at the quayside when *Offshore 1* docked. The pilot was taken to the US airbase at Bentwaters, Suffolk, where he later fully recovered. John C. Winn died in Florida on 24 August 1995, aged fifty-seven years.

'Caroline', the Song, by the Fortunes

Radio Caroline adopted the song by the Fortunes, who were managed by Radio City boss Reg Calvert.

Songwriter Tony Hiller told me in July 2014,

> I wrote the song with Perry Ford and it was released in January 1964 before Caroline came on the air. It had nothing at all to do with a radio station. Caroline was a popular girls name at the time and the Fortunes made a good recording of the song. Yes, Radio Caroline did adopt the song later and, in 1964, the BBC banned the record as they said it was promoting a pirate radio station. This helped sell the record and it has subsequently appeared on twenty-four different albums, selling in excess of a million copies. Now, fifty years later, the song is played regularly by the BBC.

'Mr Tambourine Man', The Byrds

Thanks to pirate radio, many new singers and groups became famous, too many to list here. As DJs, we had a free hand in choosing new releases. As time went on, the playlist became tightly controlled.

The Emperor Rosko (Michael Pasternak) on the air from Radio Caroline.

I clearly remember the time I received an American pressing of 'Mr Tambourine Man' by the Byrds, which had been sent to me personally from Derek Taylor, a press officer for The Beatles who was visiting the United States. I was knocked out by the arrangement of this Bob Dylan song and played it each day. Caroline House in London received dozens of phone calls from listeners who wanted to know where they could purchase it. Eventually, the record was released in Britain by CBS Records, and it became a number one hit record in July 1965. CBS gave credit to Radio Caroline in the *Daily Mail Handbook of Golden Hits*. My signature tune from then on became 'Mr Tambourine Man', but this time, an instrumental version by the Golden Gate Strings. I still use the tune today in my radio shows on the BBC.

As Radio Caroline became more popular, we received visitors to the ship. During my time with Caroline they included Graham Bonney, Dave Clark, Mike D'Abo, Guy Darrell, Adam Faith, David Garrick, Susan Hampshire, Julie Grant, Denny Laine (Moody Blues), Los Bravos, Manfred Mann, Mitch Murray, Mark Richardson, Jimmy Smith, Twinkle and Marie Vincent.

Above far left: Watching television in the mess room of the *Mi Amigo*. DJ Robbie Dale is standing on the left and Rosko is seated centre.

Below far left: Extrovert American DJ, Emperor Rosko, kept a Mynah bird, Alfie, on board.

Above and below left: Mealtime on the *Mi Amigo*. DJs included are Rick Dane, Tom Lodge and Robbie Dale.

Right: DJ Emperor Rosko at the door connecting the radio studio to the mess room, asking Rick Dane (*seated*) and Tom Lodge for a refill.

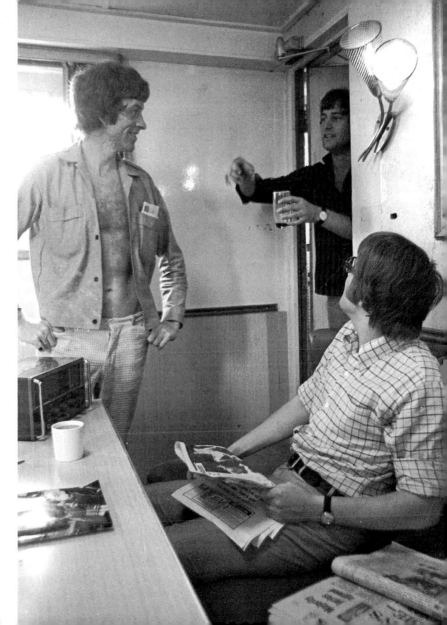

Lifeboat Drill

As Radio Caroline was at sea for 365 days a year, all of us on board had to take part in lifeboat drill. The captain would spring lifeboat drill on us at varying times. All those not on-air were expected to take part. Captain Peter Klokkers was a stickler for discipline. He told us it was important to know all about rowing and sailing, should the engine of the lifeboat either break down or run out of fuel.

During the lifeboat drill, the Dutch crew would lower one of her two lifeboats and, once aboard, Dutchmen, disc jockeys and engineers sped off to some unknown destination. The engine was stopped and we took to the oars. This was fun during the summer months, but in winter it wasn't too appealing.

The lifeboat drill was instilled in all of us, so when new DJs came on board they would be told about it soon after their arrival. In the winter of 1965, Australian Norman St John joined us as a DJ.

On his first day on board, he went to bed about 10.00 p.m. We told the captain of our intention to hold an imaginary lifeboat drill about midnight. He went along with the idea, providing we did not launch the lifeboat.

Having just spent eight days on Radio City and, prior to that, as an entertainer on passenger ships for twelve months going between Italy and Australia, I presumed Norman would be used to a 'lifeboat drill', so the following idea was born.

At midnight, engineer George Saunders woke up Norman and told him the lifeboat drill was about to take place and for him to put on his lifejacket and be on the top deck within two minutes.

Nearly fifty years later, Norman still remembers the occasion:

I was only wearing my pajamas, a thick sweater and a lifejacket. Someone shouted to me to hold the wheel of the lifeboat until such time I was told to release it. I had to put great pressure on the wheel. It was a very cold night and my hands were completely frozen. It was completely dark and everyone appeared to have disappeared. I must have been there for over half an hour, tried to attract someone's attention, but with no success. I then decided to go back to my cabin. En route I opened another DJ's door – Skues, I think it was – and said 'What the **** is going on?'

Norman was then let into the secret. He took his 'initiation' very well, and it was not too long before he was administrating his discipline on other new DJs coming aboard.

The next morning, Norman took a look on deck and saw that the wheel he had been holding so tightly, while his hands were frozen, was in fact rusted solid and had not been turned in years. It was not even part of the ship's safety equipment.

Caroline Bell Awards

To mark its first birthday, the station announced the winners of the Caroline Bell Award for the best records and artistes for the year 1964/65 in four categories.

Right: The crew of the *Mi Amigo* on the deck of the refitted ship in April 1966, as the tender pulls alongside. The ship's anchor chain is fixed alongside by ropes. Along with the ship's crew are Patrick Starling (*left*), a transmitter engineer, and DJ Tom Lodge (*third left*). One of the ship's lifeboats is at the top of the picture.

Petula Clark won her award for the best female recording artiste for her version of 'Downtown'. She was presented with her Bell by disc jockey Simon Dee on 28 March 1965, Caroline's birthday. Pet had flown in from Paris for twelve hours to record a BBC television programme. The presentation was made in the Park West offices of her British agent, Alan A. Freeman.

The award for the best and most consistent artists went to The Beatles, and Simon Dee made the presentation on 6 April 1965 at Twickenham film studios, where the four Lancashire lads were filming *Help!*

The Animals received Radio Caroline's first birthday Bell Award at London Airport as they left for New York. The presentation, made by Ronan O'Rahilly, was for the best group record of the year – 'House of the Rising Sun'.

The award for the best male vocal of the year was made to Tom Jones, for his record 'It's Not Unusual' by composer and orchestra leader Burt Bacharach on 26 April.

Talking to the author about the pirates in a radio programme on Radio Hallam in April 1987, Tom said,

Radio Caroline made a hit out of 'It's Not Unusual'. They played it a long time before the BBC picked up on it. I still have the Radio Caroline award, which is a fine brass bell on a wooden trestle. Had Caroline and the other pirate stations not been as adventurous as they were maybe BBC pop radio may never have seen the light of day.

Left: Canadian Mel Howard was a DJ on Caroline in 1965.

Caroline Good Guys

On 24 May 1965, Radio Caroline adopted the 'Good Guys' image, which was styled on radio stations WMCA in New York, and 2SM in Sydney, Australia. The idea was to abandon the term 'disc jockey', and to go out and encourage good will and courtesy in all programmes and personal appearances. We all wore identical clothing that consisted of blue-and-white check shirts, light grey trousers and double-breasted mod style yachting jacket. There were two shifts of disc jockeys ... er ... 'good guys'. Shift A consisted of Bryan Vaughan, Don Allen, Jon Sydney and Keith Skues. Shift B had Garry Kemp, Mike Allen, Tony Blackburn and Bob Walton.

While on shore leave, we fulfilled personal appearances, met pop stars and groups and discussed programme ideas at Caroline House.

Unfortunately, changes were being made. Shore leave was reduced by 50 per cent, and there was talk of cutting pay to those on the ships. The programme format of music changed. DJ Don Allen was transferred from the south to north ship and, in August and September 1965, a number of seasoned broadcasters lost their jobs. They were Doug Kerr, Garry Kemp, Mike Allen, Roger Gale and Jon Sydney. Three more resigned in December 1965: Bryan Vaughan, Paul Noble and myself.

Bryan Vaughan joined Radio Scotland, and Paul Noble travelled out to the Caribbean and worked for Radio Antilles. In my case, I had been offered a job on land-based Radio

Right: Keith Skues in the record library of Radio Caroline, on board the *Mi Amigo* in 1965.

Luxembourg, presenting the CBS 'Record Show' and appearing in a Southern Television pop show. On Radio Caroline I had begun with a salary of £12 a week. By the time I left, it had gone up to £20 a week. The Radio Luxembourg show was paying a guinea a minute. To use a slang expression I was 'quids in'.

With this upheaval, Tom Lodge, who had proved to be a popular disc jockey on Radio Caroline North, was parachuted in to take over as programme director of the south ship in October 1965. He brought with him Mike Ahern, and took on new boys Emperor Rosko, Graham Webb, Robbie Dale and Keith Hampshire. Norman St John and Tony Blackburn remained in place … for the time being. They later joined Radio London, as did a certain 'Cardboard Shoes'.

Tom Lodge was the grandson of Sir Oliver Lodge, who played an important part in the development of wireless telegraphy. He told the disc jockeys he wanted positive attitude, commitment and involvement, and planned to change the South ship's musical output to the uptempo, carefree sound of the North ship. Furthermore, he wanted to win over the listeners who were tuning in to Radio London, which attracted a huge audience.

Radio Caroline South Runs Aground

On 20 January 1966, the MV *Mi Amigo* lost its anchor, drifted and ran aground on a wave-lashed Great Holland beach at

Left: Paul Noble worked for Caroline from January to December 1965.

Chevaux de Frise Point. The station had ceased broadcasting the night before. On board the ship were Captain Willy Wrury and an eight-man crew with disc jockeys Tom Lodge, Tony Blackburn, Graham Webb, Norman St John and Dave Lee Travis. Engineers were Carl Thomson, George Saunders and Patrick Starling. Wearing his famous trilby hat, Norman St John was the first person to be brought ashore by breeches buoy. Now resident in Brisbane, Australia, he will never forget the rescue:

> I had gone to bed around 11 o'clock but was awakened to find the captain giving orders for us to put on warm clothing and life jackets as we might have to abandon ship. There was a Force 9 gale blowing. The ship's spotlight revealed that we were only about 30 yards from a concrete wall on the beach. Moments later, the ship that built up a name all around the world as one of Britain's first pirate radio stations was aground. Realising the danger of the ship breaking up, coastguards at this time fired rockets with ropes attached in order to fix the breeches buoy. The first rocket missed and exploded on the deck of the *Mi Amigo*, but the second was successful. We then formed an orderly queue and prepared to leave the ship.

Had we known about his television challenge in the Australian jungle thirty-six years later, Tony Blackburn might well have said 'I'm a Celebrity. Get Me Out of Here'. While filming an item for BBC TV's *Inside Out* in January 1966, Tony told me he was awoken in the early hours of 20 January and thought it was a joke:

> Norman St John told me to go on deck. As I was on the 'Breakfast Show' I told him to go away as I needed all the sleep I could get. Eventually the captain came down to say we really were in trouble. I went on deck to find car headlights and houses on the shore coming nearer and nearer. It was cold and dark. We had missed the television warning. Waves were crashing over the ship and there was this terrible crunching sound as she ran aground.

Once everyone had been rescued, they were taken first to Frinton Golf Club House, and then to Walton-on-the-Naze police station where they were given a change of clothing and cups of tea all round.

On the beach, a desperate race against time and tide to save Caroline was made throughout the night and following day. There were fears the *Mi Amigo* would break up, or be flung against the sea wall. At 11 a.m. on 21 January, Caroline freed herself from the beach. Within an hour, the Coast Rescue Company had retrieved all their kit from the beach and stood down at noon, as did Walton Coastguards. The *Mi Amigo* was towed by the tug *Titan* to IJmuiden, and then up the North Sea Canal to Zaandam, a town close to Amsterdam.

On 22 January 1966, Ronan O'Rahilly received a message from Mrs Britt Wadner of Radio Syd in Sweden, offering him the radio ship *Cheetah II*. Ronan was most grateful for this expression of unity and accepted her kind offer.

The *Cheetah II*, built in Norway in 1924, housed the Danish station Radio Mercur from 1962. In January, she sailed from the Baltic, arrived off the British shores, and was guided into position where the *Mi Amigo* normally anchored.

Disc jockey Colin Nichol, now resident in Perth, Western Australia, still has vivid memories of the time the *Cheetah II* became a temporary home for Radio Caroline South:

My first impressions were that she looked a homely kind of ship and the atmosphere on board was very relaxed. Even now, forty-eight years later, I can feel the friendliness and homely warmth that seemed to characterise the old Baltic ferry. I had the feeling that many people, over many years, had enjoyed being aboard her … and I knew that I was to feel more relaxed and at home on the *Cheetah II* that I had felt on board ship ever before.

On 12 February 1966, after a break of less than a month, Caroline South was back on the air. Colin went on:

That other great innovator of shipboard broadcasting, the Dutch Radio Veronica, must also not be forgotten as central to the innovations that resulted in the advent of British offshore radio. More than a generation later, they are all still well remembered, and missed.

It may have been a comfortable ship, but technically the station was off-air more than on-air. This annoyed the DJs, and two of them – Tony Blackburn and Norman St John – were heard swearing in separate incidents. Both thought they were off-air at the time. Wrong! Listeners were more amused than annoyed.

The *Mi Amigo* returned from her refitting in April 1966. While the *Mi Amigo* was in Holland, a brand new 50 kilowatt Continental Electronics transmitter was installed, the studios were renovated, the aerial mast extended and a new generator fitted.

Transmissions began on 25 April on a new frequency of 253 metres medium wave. Presenters used the call sign 259 to rhyme with Caroline.

A Wedding Ceremony on MV *Caroline*

A wedding took place on board ship on 20 September 1966, when a disc jockey was married on board. Both aged twenty-three, Mick Luvzit was married to pretty, auburn-haired Janet Teret, in a ceremony performed by the ship's Dutch captain, Martin Gipps. The MV *Caroline* was registered in Panama, so it made the marriage ceremony quite legal.

Mick wore a black velvet jacket, yellow cravat, pinstriped trousers and high-heeled Chelsea boots. The bride was delayed by two hours because of fog. She arrived by motor launch, wearing hipster slacks with a nine-inch bare midriff. She was barefoot with her toenails painted crimson. This was certainly a mod wedding with a difference! The ten-minute ceremony was broadcast live on Radio Caroline to an estimated 4 million listeners. The best man was Ray Teret, the bride's brother, who was a former Radio Caroline disc jockey. Mick and Janet, who later had a daughter Jelisse, were divorced in the 1970s and Mick returned to Canada. He died following heart surgery on 8 December 2012, aged seventy.

Shore Leave

Shore leave was always something to which we looked forward. From the Caroline South ship, we would catch the tender back to Harwich or Felixstowe. Normally, we were delayed by HM Customs, who checked each one of us to ensure we were not bringing back any alcohol or cigarettes.

The *Mi Amigo* aground at Chevaux de Friese
Point, Holland-on-Sea, Essex, in January 1966.

Above: Ronan O'Rahilly (*centre*) watching with police and coastguards as the *Mi Amigo* was being refloated from the beach at Holland-on-Sea in 1966.

Right: A shipwrecked Tony Blackburn, still wearing his lifejacket, recovering with a cup of tea.

Left: Radio Caroline's liaison officer Bill Scadden (*third right*), with the shipwrecked Radio Caroline team outside the Portobello Hotel, Walton-on-the-Naze, Essex, the morning after the disaster. Pictured, from left: Carl Thompson, Norman St John, Patrick Starling, Tony Blackburn, Thys Spyker, Graham Webb, Tom Lodge, Bill Scadden, Dave Lee Travis and George Saunders.

Left: A member of the coastguard team waves as the *Mi Amigo* as it makes its way into deeper water.

Above: A crowd of mostly elderly onlookers gathered on the sea wall at Holland-on-Sea to see the *Mi Amigo* being refloated.

Above right: The *Cheeta II* off Essex in 1966. The coastline is in the background.

Above far right: Colin Nichol (*left*) Britt Wadner and Ronan O'Rahilly with the Caroline bell on board the *Cheetah II*. The ship came on the air with test broadcasts on 12 February 1966, programming started the following day.

Below far right: Just how close the *Mi Amigo* was to being totally wrecked, after being swept onto the beach close to a concrete groin at Holland-on-Sea, is illustrated as the ship was refloated.

Below right: Ronan O'Rahilly (*centre*) watches as the tender *Offshore 1* lifts the ships anchor from the deck of the *Mi Amigo* to drop it to the seabed.

Above left: The refitted *Mi Amigo* returned to the Essex coast on 5 April 1966, after a refit at Zaandam, Holland. The ship had been fitted with a new 50 kilowatt transmitter. Programming started from the *Mi Amigo* on 24 April 1966.

Above: Ronan O'Rahilly and Britt Wadner in one of the radio studios on the *Cheetah II* in January 1966. Photographer David Kindred remembers:

I made the trip from Harwich on the tender *Offshore 1* with Ronan O'Rahilly, Britt Wadner and Colin Nichol to find the *Cheetah II* off the Essex coast in thick fog. It took hours to find each other with the visibility down to a few yards. The sounding of ship hooters eventually solved the problem. The tender left us on the *Cheetah* and sailed to service Radio London. The Dutch crew of the tender forgot about us and returned to port! Ronan took charge, serving soup when the Swedish crew made us an evening meal. We eventually got back to land around midnight.

Left: A rare moment when Ronan O'Rahilly sat at the mixing desk on the *Mi Amigo,* when the ship returned in 1966 from the refit in Holland.

Above: Transmitter engineer Patrick Starling, with the new 50 kilowatt transmitter on the *Mi Amigo* in April 1966.

Above right: The 50 kilowatt transmitter in the hold of the *Mi Amigo* in 1966.

Right: Ronan O'Rahilly (*second left*) and DJ Tom Lodge (*second right*) with members of the Dutch crew on the *Mi Amigo*.

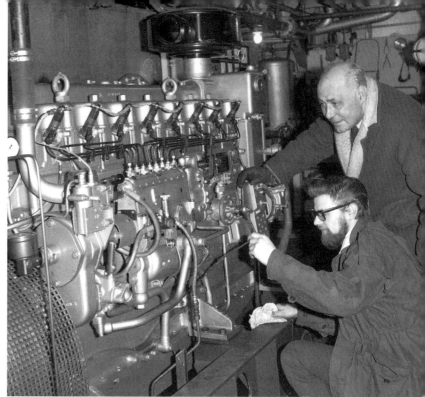

Above: Bill Scadden (*top*) and an engineer with a brand new generator on the *Mi Amigo*, after the 1966 refit in Holland.

Left: A thumbs up for the crew of the *Mi Amigo* from Ronan O'Rahilly in April 1966. (*Photograph by Alf Smith*)

Coming ashore from two weeks on a small ship that tossed and turned, pitched and rolled, it was rather strange to stand on solid ground. It seemed that the pavement was coming up to meet you. The legs and feet felt very heavy. It took a few hours to feel comfortable walking on solid ground again.

The journey back to London was either by train or our own car. Normally there would be about twenty or thirty people waiting for us at Harwich. Cars would be parked in lay-bys and would follow us, eventually overtaking and finally waving us down to request a 'freebie' record. When we drove through big towns like Colchester, Chelmsford, Brentwood, Romford and Ilford, there were always people lying in wait.

On other occasions, we would return to London by train. Earlier in the day, we had broadcast that a number of us would be going on shore leave for a week. We asked listeners to be at a particular railway station so we could all have a quick chat from the carriage window. On one Monday, in November 1965, there were so many people who had come to the platforms at Manningtree, Colchester and Chelmsford that the train arrived at Liverpool Street, London, twenty minutes late. British Rail were not amused. Neither were many passengers who had other trains to connect.

As disc jockeys, we were truly honoured that listeners would show us such friendliness. We were out at sea broadcasting fun to a large audience. At the same time, I hope it proved to them that we were not stuffy individuals no one ever saw, but humans with whom you could have a conversation.

Arrival of Radio London

By Christmas 1964, the idea of broadcasting pop music to Britain from just outside the control of the authorities had started to spread. A powerful American-financed station Radio London (also known as 'Big L'), on board a former American Navy minesweeper USS *Density*, now renamed MV *Galaxy*, dropped anchor close to Caroline on 5 December 1964.

Paul Kaye was the very first (and last) voice to be heard on Radio London on 23 December 1964: 'Good morning ladies and gentlemen. This is Radio London transmitting in the medium wave band on 266 metres – 1133 kilocycles at a power of 50 kilowatts.' In fact, the station began on 17 kilowatts and went to full power on 20 March 1965. Pete Brady presented the first breakfast show, where he told listeners that they would be broadcasting the station's Top 40 records – later to be called 'The Fab 40.' His first record was by Cliff Richard – 'I Could Easily Fall in Love With You'. The records played on Radio London tended to be about six weeks ahead of the national charts. There was a format to a radio programme: Top 40, new release, LP tracks and revived 45s. There was a strict rotation to which DJs had to adhere.

Managing director of Radio London was Philip Birch, thirty-seven, who had his offices at 17 Curzon Street, London, just around the corner from Radio Caroline in Chesterfield Gardens. The station started with a capital of £500,000, of which some was American money and some British. It cost £15,000 a month to run the station.

Where did the idea of Radio London originate? The answer was Eastland, Texas, USA, where, in 1964, businessman

Don Pierson, owner of Abilene National Bank, had been installed as mayor of the city. He had visited London on a number of occasions and noted how dull British radio sounded in comparison to American radio. Pierson had seen a newspaper article about Ronan O'Rahilly's plans to launch a commercial radio ship off the English coast. He was convinced it could be a good financial investment. He met with a number of colleagues and all agreed it could make a profitable enterprise.

For the first time, Britain had Top 40 format radio staffed with largely more experienced DJs, some from America and Australia, where commercial Top 40 stations were well established. The sound of the station was completely different to Radio Caroline. The presentation was styled on KLIF Radio, an American Top 40 station broadcasting to Dallas, Texas. It was somewhat toned down for the benefit of British listeners.

On board the *Galaxy*, anchored 3½ miles off Frinton-on-Sea, Essex, there were twenty-two men who controlled the ship twenty-four hours a day. She had a Dutch captain, and a crew of twelve, who worked three weeks on board and a week in Holland. Disc jockeys and engineers worked two weeks on board, with a week in London.

The *Galaxy* (780 tons, dead weight 1,100 tons) was a former United States minesweeper, USS *Density*, that served in the Far East in the Second World War, and was 180 feet in length and 33 feet wide. As Radio London, she comprised a flying bridge, the bridge deck, the main deck and the studio deck.

As well as all the latest pop tunes, Radio London broadcast news bulletins. News editor Paul Kaye reported,

We decided to present a news service at half past every hour. It is a known fact that listeners who hear nothing but music acquire a guilt complex at not being well informed. Secondly, they might decide to seek this information from other sources – namely the BBC Light Programme.

Radio London was the first offshore station to incorporate news in their schedules, and was later followed by Radios Caroline, City, 390 and other stations.

There were two messes – one for disc jockeys and engineers and the other for the Dutch crew. The captain, chief engineer and mate used the DJs' mess, which, during wartime, was the war room. Each of the messes had a television set that could pick up transmission from BBC and ITV (Anglia).

On the studio deck was the record library, which housed some 5,000 singles and 500 LPs. Beyond the library were the studios. When transmissions began in December 1964, there was just one studio comprising two 16-inch Gates turntables, three RCA cartridge machines, an Ampex tape machine and a Scully tape reproducer. Mixing facilities were provided by an RCA four-channel mixer.

Having served on Radio Caroline South, followed by a stint on Radio Luxembourg, I joined Radio London in the spring of 1966, just at the time that engineer Martin Newton built an additional studio incorporating a ten-channel mixing console with quadrant faders and duplicate equipment that had been installed in studio one. It was to become the main on-air studio.

A ride on the tender for Dave Lee Travis back to land in 1965. The Radio London ship, *Galaxy*, is in the background.

Left: Emperor Rosko (*centre*) and Tom Lodge, along with members of the ship's crew on the deck of the *Mi Amigo*. A photograph taken from the tender.

Right: A tender brings supplies on a warm summer's day in 1966.

Pop Singers Visit the MV *Galaxy*

Among many guest stars that visited the *Galaxy* during her stint off the Essex coast were Gene Pitney, Spencer Davis, Marianne Faithfull, Guy Darrell, Twice as Much, Barry Benson, Geno Washington, Frank Ifield, David Garrick, Normie Rowe and P. P. Arnold.

When we met in 1968, at Broadcasting House, London, Gene Pitney, who had twenty-one hit records in the British charts, remembered his visit to the *Galaxy*:

I was shown around the ship and interviewed on-air. In all I took about five rolls of film, including the inside of DJs cabins. It was something I had wanted to do ever since I learned of the British pirate radio ships. I travelled out in June 1965, from Harwich. On board the *Offshore 1* was a member of the Royal Family, Prince Richard. (now the present Duke of Gloucester). Although the weather was rough, it was a most memorable day.

Gene Pitney was on a UK tour when he was found dead in his Hilton Hotel room hotel in Cardiff on 5 April 2006. He was sixty-six years old.

Another American, P. P. Arnold, who was one of the backing voices on the Ike and Tina Turner hit record 'River Deep Mountain High', had a Top 20 hit record of her own with 'The First Cut is the Deepest'. She visited Radio London in 1967. I interviewed her on Classic Gold Radio in 1990 and she recalled,

As an American I had heard a lot about the British pirate radio stations. They were very popular and played records that listeners

wanted to hear. I was invited out to the ship in April 1967. The journey out on the tender was traumatic and the time we had reached the Radio London ship I was feeling ill as the sea was very choppy. But the disc jockeys made me very welcome. Radio London helped my record become a national Top 20 hit in May 1967.

The Tremeloes celebrated their first British chart topper by visiting the *Galaxy* on 15 May 1967. They appeared on-air and thanked Radio London for their support. Without Radio London's help, they would not have been number one nationally in the charts on that day with the record 'Silence is Golden', penned by American songwriters Bob Crewe and Bob Gaudio.

On 8 June, Lord and Lady Arran paid a courtesy visit to Radio London. They had lunch on board with disc jockeys and later were interviewed on-air. Lord Arran said, after his visit, 'My wife and I had a wonderful day and we were delighted to see everyone on board so very happy. I like seeing contented people in a community, and pop radio has brought a great deal of joy to many people.'

Radio London promoted new groups, songwriters, record producers and independent record labels that emerged at the time. Miki Dallon became established during the Radio London days. He remembers,

A lot of us can look back to the pirates and thank them for where we are today. They were more progressive than the BBC

Left: The MV *Galaxy* moored of Frinton-on-Sea in December 1964. This photograph was taken a week before Radio London came on the air.

stations, and always trying to find something new to identify with the public. When you look at the business nowadays, you realise just how talented they were in picking individuals like me, who couldn't get the break into the BBC. Radio London, and stations like that, gave everyone with some talent a chance. I had written a song called 'That's Nice', which I gave to an unknown singer called Neil Christian to record. We gave a copy to Radio London. They liked it and played it regularly. It made the Top 20 nationally in April 1966.

Singer Jimmy Ruffin remembers he met a number of the pirate DJs on a promotional visit to England in the summer of 1966. They played a lot of Tamla Motown records in their programmes. I know they helped make my record, 'What Becomes of the Broken Hearted', a hit in October 1966.

Radio London did help make hit records. An example was 'Winchester Cathedral', by the New Vaudeville Band. The group who produced the record had never done anything before. It was brought into 'The Fab 40'. The listeners loved the record, and it became one of the biggest selling records not just in the UK but all over the world

A record that sold more than 6 million copies happened through Denny Cordell, who formed a new company and, with the help of music publisher David Platz of Essex, found an outlet for his productions. 'One of the records I was contracted to record was "A Whiter Shade of Pale" by Procol Harum. It was released on the newly formed Deram label, went to the top of the charts in June 1967. It remained in the charts for fifteen weeks.'

Christmas on Board 'Big L'

Normally at Christmastime, married disc jockeys and engineers were allowed to spend time with their families. For those of us who were single there was a great atmosphere on board. The messes were bedecked with Christmas trees, thousands of Christmas cards from listeners and countless decorations. The broadcasting side of the station carried on twenty-four hours a day.

I was fortunate to work over the 1966 festivities, along with fellow disc jockeys Tony Windsor, Ed Stewart, Mike Lennox, Kenny Everett and Chuck Blair, administrator Richard Swainson and engineers Dave Hawkins and Russell Tollerfield.

Our Christmas dinner, served at 1800 hours, included apéritif with a little snack; hors d'oeuvre variés, wine; consommé julienne; bouchée à la reine; canard à la orange with sauce, pommes noisette, allumettes; orange fruit, Christmas pudding and finally café, ase fromages, and brandy.

April Fool's Day, 1967

One of the most memorable days aboard *Galaxy* was 1 April 1967, when we decided to do an April Fool. Morning transmissions from 'Big L' were interrupted by Radio East Anglia, allegedly broadcasting from a disused signal box on the railway line between King's Lynn and Norwich. Two of Radio London's engineers, Dave Hawkins and Ian West, pretended they were a new station operating on 267 metres, with a signal so powerful that it almost obliterated 'Big L'. Gerry Bishop mentions the event in his 1975 book *Offshore Radio*:

The Radio London ship MV *Galaxy* from the supply tender in the summer of 1966.

As the morning progressed, test transmissions from Radio East Anglia continued, interrupting not only the records but commercials and news as well. The 10.30 a.m. Radio London news should have enabled listeners to deduce what was going on. Lead item concerned the extension of Felixstowe Pier to 3 miles, so that offshore stations would be brought within the 3-mile limit, and there followed a number of other fake items including an impossible weather forecast. Just before noon, Radio London faded in and Radio East Anglia was never heard again. The whole thing had been broadcast from the *Galaxy* by clever mixing and very good production work.

I have to plead guilty here as I was 51 per cent responsible for the hoax. Ed Stewart was 49 per cent responsible, as we had to interrupt his show.

Ed Stewart, in his 2005 book *Out of the Stewpot*, says,

> Managing director Philip Birch and programme director Alan Keen were going bananas whilst listening in their respective homes. Keen was not best pleased and had even thought of firing both Keith Skues and myself, the perpetrators of this heinous crime. What saved us was the immense publicity we received in the press, which resulted in an extra awareness of the station.

Now, forty-seven years later, this is where I plead forgiveness from David Kindred, then working as a photographer with the *Ipswich Evening Star*. He was travelling out to the Radio London ship the day of the hoax. What he did not know was that we gave out his home address to where irate fans could write and complain. And they did. Dave remembers,

It was a great surprise when I boarded the Radio London ship that day and Keith played me a recording of the hoax, with my home address as the base of Radio East Anglia. I had been on the tender for two hours where it was too noisy to listen to the radio.

I thought it was a huge joke and saw it as a clear April Fool stunt. My mother was even more surprised. She knew nothing of this as I was out on the North Sea. A staff reporter from a Sunday newspaper knocked on the door and was not convinced by my mother's denials. He stepped back, looked up for a transmitting aerial, and said 'Are you sure you are not transmitting from here madam?' Sorry Mum!

Radio London, a Top 40 Station with a Personality of its Own

Philip Birch, managing director of Radio London, told me in an interview in August 1974, that he felt that if a commercial station was to succeed, the first thing was to attract a very large audience, so that advertisers would be keen to support it to deliver their sales message on-air. 'So the station had to do something entirely different. Not just a pop station, but a pop station with a personality of its own.'

Borrowed from American radio, it adopted the Top 40 format, the only idea being to play the forty records that were the most interesting records of the week. It bore no resemblance to the national music charts. DJs would select forty records collectively – what they thought were the best forty records of the week – and that would be the sound of the station for the following seven days. Philip Birch went on,

The station had to be professional. We wanted Radio London to move very fast in a happy way and for the listener to feel that the station itself was dynamic and alive. We did this by using jingles, which had not been used by anyone very much until that time. We introduced the jingle 'Wonderful Radio London'. In 1967, BBC Radio 1 introduced a series of jingles based on the Radio London package and using the slogan 'Wonderful Radio 1'. The whole pace of Radio London was rapid, but pleasant.

Philip Birch said that while the station was on-air for two-and-a-half years, it was never involved in any litigation:

We were absolute model citizens in every way. We had very strict rules with our staff, who realised we were broadcasting outside the law rather than against it, and that we behaved ourselves and ran our organisation in a model way. We paid a Performing Right copyright fee for the music. We offered to pay Phonographic Performance Limited, another royalty organisation, but they were not prepared to accept our money. Pirate radio was great fun. We did something very worthwhile and for which we can be proud.

New Arrivals Radio England and Britain Radio – Two Radio Stations on One Ship

Known as 'Swinging Radio England' and 'Britain Radio', the stations came on-air in June 1966, operating from the MV *Olga Patricia*, later renamed MV *Laissez-Faire*. She had been a Second World War Liberty ship of 480 tons. The two stations used a transmitter, with a joint power of 110 kilowatts.

Radio England began test transmissions in May, with regular programmes from 18 June 1966. Britain Radio, 'Hallmark of Quality', began broadcasting the following day. Radio England transmitted on 227 metres medium wave; Britain Radio on 355 metres. The cost of launching both stations was estimated at £1.45 million.

A widely publicised champagne party for both stations took place in the autumn of 1966 at the Hilton Hotel, where hundreds of guests made an appearance, including Dusty Springfield, Tom Jones, Small Faces, Dave Berry, Neil Christian, Chris Farlowe, Walker Brothers, Dave Clark Five, John Lennon, Sandie Shaw, Herman's Hermits, Moody Blues, Alma Cogan, Alan Price, Paul and Barry Ryan, Geno Washington and many more household names. On 14 March 1967, Peir-Vick Ltd, the company that backed the stations, went broke to the tune of £110,000. That was some kind of party!

Both stations transmitted their programmes through two separate aerials, held aloft by a 210-foot mast. Although the pop station was called Radio England, the DJs were mainly American, and they tended to shout at their audience rather than talking to them – while acceptable in the United States of America, we were in Great Britain. The station lacked advertising, lacked support from shareholders and, finally, suffered loss of support from her listeners.

Following the closure of Radio England, the *Laissez-Faire* transmitted a programme in Dutch under the station name Radio Dolfijn. Commencing transmissions in November 1966, she changed her call sign to Radio 227 in March 1967, and closed down on 21 July 1967.

Chuck Blair joined Radio England in July 1966 and later transferred to Radio London, until its closure in August 1967.

Willy Walker joined Radio London as a DJ in May 1966, and was with the station until closure in August 1967.

Radio London DJ John Peel in 1967. He later joined BBC Radio 1 and became a national name on television and radio. He died in October 2004, while on holiday in Peru.

Above left: The tender, *Offshore 1*, sailing from Felixstowe Dock in the summer of 1967, with Philip Birch, managing director of Radio London, on board to break the bad news of the end of the station to the staff on the *Galaxy*.

Above: DJ Norman St John in the broadcast studio of Radio London in 1966.

Left: Philip Birch (*centre*), the managing director of Radio London, on board the tender *Offshore 1* at Felixstowe Dock in 1967. Mr Birch was on his way to the ship to tell staff that the station would go off the air a few weeks later on 14 August 1967. On the left is DJ Tony Brandon and radio engineer Mike Howell, the chief engineer in charge of the Radio London transmitters.

Britain Radio began transmission on 19 June 1966. The format of programmes was aimed at the housewife and broadcast 'middle of the road' music from artists like Dean Martin, Tony Bennett, Frank Sinatra, Percy Faith, Ray Conniff, Johnny Mathis and Peggy Lee.

Although very popular, Britain Radio failed to attract both audiences and revenue. She closed down on 22 February 1967 and was replaced by Radio 355. Its operation was short-lived and the station ceased broadcasting on 5 August 1967.

More New Floating Radio Stations

Radio 270

Radio 270 (which broadcast on 270 metres, 1,115 kilocycles) adopted the Top 40 format similar to Radio London's, but called it the Fun 40. They broadcast hourly news bulletins, sports flashes, weather forecasts and community announcements.

Based on board *Oceaan 7*, off Scarborough, the station was very popular in the Yorkshire, Humberside, Northumberland and Tyneside areas. It was a late starter, commencing broadcasting on 4 June 1966, and it closed down at midnight on 14 August 1967, the last possible moment before the government's Marine Offences Bill became law.

Right: The *Laissez-Faire*, formally the *Olga Patricia*, home of Radio England, Britain Radio, Radio Dolfijn, Radio 277 and Radio 355. This photograph was taken in July 1967.

Radio 355 DJs at Felixstowe Dock in August 1967 soon after the station closed. They are, from left: John Aston, Martin Kayne, Tony Windsor, Tony Monson, Alan Black and Mark Sloane.

Radio Scotland

Broadcasting from the *Comet*, a former lightship, the station began broadcasting at Hogmanay, as the bells were bringing in the New Year 1966. Radio Scotland transmitted on 242 metres, 1,241 kHz, later adjusted to 1,259 kHz but retaining its 242 identification. It was a very popular station among listeners.

The station received a summons that was returnable at Ayr on 13 March 1967, where it was fined £80 for transmitting within territorial waters. Due to the Marine Offences Act coming into operation from midnight on 14 August 1967, Radio Scotland closed down at the last possible moment – midnight!

Fort Based Radio Stations (in Chronological Order)

Radio Sutch

This station was operated by pop singer and parliamentary candidate 'Screaming Lord Sutch', and began broadcasting from Shivering Sands Fort on 27 May 1964 on 197 metres, 1,542 kHz. I was working with David Sutch at a show in Scarborough in 1989 and he told me:

> The format we had on the radio station caused eyebrows to be raised, and because of the enormous depth of my political appeal, the authorities had to silence me. I was finally forced to surrender in order to avoid bloodshed. I was satisfied that I had made my point.

Radio Sutch was taken over in September 1964 by Reginald Calvert, who changed the name to Radio City.

Radio Invicta

Broadcasting on 306 metres, 985 kHz, the station, based on forts at Red Sands in the Thames Estuary, began regular broadcasting on 17 July 1964. The station closed down halfway through February 1965, and a new station, KING Radio, took over the forts on Red Sands and commenced test transmissions on 25 February 1965.

Radio City

Radio City, also known as 'The Tower of Power', first went on the air in September 1964 and was run by Reginald Calvert, who managed a number of pop groups. The station transmitted from a group of derelict forts on Shivering Sands in the Thames Estuary, on 299 metres, 1,003 kHz. Project Atlanta had put on board an extra transmitter for the new station, and owed £10,000 to Major Oliver Smedley of Project Atlanta for its erection. He intended claiming it back.

In the early hours of 20 June 1966, Smedley led a boarding party of riggers and took control of the station. After a few hours, Smedley left the fort and returned home to his Essex cottage, leaving the riggers in charge. The following evening, Reg Calvert visited Smedley at his home in Wendens Ambo, near Saffron Walden. The door was opened by Smedley's secretary/housekeeper, who did her best to stop Calvert gaining access to the cottage. A scuffle developed and Smedley appeared with a shotgun and killed Calvert.

Smedley appeared in court at Saffron Walden accused of the murder of Reg Calvert. The jury took three days to decide that no court would convict on a murder charge. He was sent for trial at Chelmsford. On 18 October, he was found not guilty of 'unlawfully' killing Reg Calvert on 21 June 1966 and was completely discharged.

Radio City was taken over by Reg Calvert's widow, Dorothy. On 8 February 1967, she appeared before magistrates at Rochford accused of operating a radio station without a licence. She said that Radio City, based on a fort at Shivering Sands, was outside territorial limits. However, the magistrates disagreed and she was fined £100. That evening the station closed down with the national anthem at midnight.

KING Radio

KING Radio began regular broadcasting from Red Sands on 9 March 1965, and was the successor to Radio Invicta. The station transmitted on 238 metres, 1,289 kHz.

Advertising revenue was very small and did not cover the running costs. The listening audience was some 20,000. After only six months on-air, the station ended broadcasting on 22 September 1965. Its successor, Radio 390, wasted no time with in its takeover and went on-air just three days later.

Radio 390

Housed on a former wartime fort, with several towers connected by catwalks, the fort known as Red Sands was located 8 miles off Whitstable in the Thames Estuary. The station went on-air on 25 September 1965, transmitting on 390 metres, 773kHz.

Radio 390 was fined £100 on 25 November 1966 after being found guilty of broadcasting without a licence. The station continued broadcasting, and were once again brought before

Left: Ian MacRea was a DJ on Radio City in 1966, which broadcast from a former anti-aircraft fort close to Kent. Ian joined Radio Caroline in 1967.

magistrates at Rochford on 22 and 23 February 1967. They were found guilty and the company fined £200.

On 28 July 1967, Radio 390 ceased broadcasting, and it ended its transmissions with all three verses of the national anthem. Two weeks later, the Marine Etc., Broadcasting (Offences) Bill became an Act of Parliament.

Red Sands was used in an episode of *Danger Man* entitled 'Not So Jolly Roger', starring Patrick McGoohan, which was broadcast on ITV in 1965. Filming had taken place while Radio 390 was in residence. External shots of the towers and superstructure were shown in the television programme.

Radio Essex

Regular programmes began from Knock John Fort in the Thames Estuary on 7 November 1965 on 222 metres, 1,353 kHz. The station received a summons to appear in court at Rochford on 30 September 1966, alleging that, on 16 August 1966, it had contravened Section One of the Wireless Telegraphy Act 1949 by operating without a licence. Radio Essex was £100 and, against the advice of its solicitors, carried on broadcasting after changing its name to Britain's Better Music Station. However, the money had run out and the station closed on Christmas Day 1966. The equipment was dismantled and taken to Roughs Tower, which was later set up as the Independent State of Sealand. No broadcasting took place from here, except for several official licensed amateur contests.

Tower Radio

Programmes commenced from Sunk Head Tower on 15 October 1965. After various test transmissions, it settled on 236 metres, 1,268 kHz. Their gimmick call sign was 'Get a fix on 236!' Transmissions ended in December 1965. There followed a name change from Radio Tower to Tower Radio, operational from 28 April 1966 to 12 May 1966.

On Friday 18 August 1967, a team of twenty Royal Engineers boarded the fort and, after several small explosions and three days work, the final charge of 2,200 pounds of explosive was set. Having checked first that no one was living on the fort, they blew up Sunk Head Tower in the afternoon of 22 August. A vivid crimson flash was seen, followed by a large cloud of smoke. Large chunks of concrete flew into the air, some landing over half a mile away. The heat and force of the blast was felt on Walton-on-the-Naze beach, some 14 miles away. All that remains of the fort today are the stumps of the legs, which are still used as navigational aids to shipping entering the Thames Estuary.

Caroline Defies Authority

The shooting of Reg Calvert of Radio City on 22 June 1966 sped up the government's decision to take action to outlaw the offshore radio stations.

Hugh Jenkins, a Labour MP for Putney, said in the House of Commons on 23 June 1966 that there had been a tendency to dismiss pirate radio as a matter of no great importance. The extraordinary and tragic events of the past twenty-four hours had perhaps confirmed to everybody – the opposition as well as the government – that piracy was piracy, in whatever aspect it occurred.

The Marine Etc., Broadcasting (Offences) Bill was finally introduced into the House of Commons on 27 July 1966,

Left: The Sunk Head Fort off the Essex coast was home to Tower Radio, run by Colchester, Essex, businessman Eric Sullivan from 22 October 1965 until April 1966. The station was low powered and not often on the air. The fort was built as part of the anti-aircraft defences in the Thames Estuary during the Second World War and was then operated by the Royal Navy. The Knock John Fort further south, and of the same design, was used by Radio Essex from October 1965 until October 1966. The radio equipment was moved by owner Roy Bates to another similar fort, The Roughs Tower, off Felixstowe, Suffolk. It is home to the claimed Independent State of Sealand. Another design of fort, Red Sands, in the estuary, was first used by Radio Invicta from 29 July 1964, this was taken over by King Radio in February 1965. On 25 September 1965, Radio 390 took over the fort. This station was highly successful, transmitting a unique sweet music format. The Shivering Sands Fort was used by Radio Sutch from 27 May 1964. The station was taken over by Radio City in September 1964. Radio City closed 9 February 1967.

Below left: The tug *Collies* alongside the Sunk Head Fort, as Royal Engineers prepare to blow up the Second World War fort in August 1967. (*Photograph East Anglian Daily Times*)

Right: The Sunk Head fort off the Essex coast was destroyed by the Royal Engineers in August 1967. It was blown up to stop any further use of the abandoned structure. (*Photograph East Anglian Daily Times*)

just twenty-eight months after the offshore stations began broadcasting off the British coasts.

The UK Labour Government enacted the Bill that became an Act of Parliament, coming into effect at midnight on 14 August 1967. It outlawed advertising on or supplying unlicensed offshore radio stations from the British Isles. The maximum penalty for all these offences were the same – two years imprisonment, or a fine determined by the court, or both.

Many debates took place in the House of Commons between 1964 and 1967, when the government had claimed that the offshore radio stations were a danger because of radio interference to emergency shipping channels. Also that none of the stations were paying royalties to British copyright bodies.

All the offshore stations closed down before the Act came into force. All but one!

Radio Caroline defied the government and continued to broadcast under their new name Radio Caroline International. At midnight on 14 August, both ships played the civil rights song 'We Shall Overcome'. DJs Johnnie Walker (who joined the station from Swinging Radio England in October 1966) and Robbie Dale sang along with the chorus. Both said farewell to England and chose to live in Holland for at least three years. Johnnie's final announcement was, 'You have our assurance that we shall carry on, because we belong to you, and we love you.' The Beatles' record 'All You Need Is Love' followed, and the programme carried on through the night.

Robbie Dale said, 'Both Johnnie and I wanted to be the first to make a broadcast when we became criminals at midnight, so we have split the midnight programme so we can both do it.'

Up in the north, anti-offshore legislation covered the Isle of Man two weeks later than on the mainland, because the islands' parliament, The Tynwald, did not wish to pass the Marine Offences Act, but it was forced on them by an Order in Council.

The Caroline supply operation moved to the Netherlands, a country that did not introduce legislation until 1974. Their offshore station, Radio Veronica, had been broadcasting to Holland from the *Borkum Riff*, anchored in international waters off Katwijk aan Zee, from 21 April 1960. In 1964, the *Borkum Riff* was towed into harbour and broken up. It was replaced by the *Norderney*. The station continued to broadcast until 31 August 1974, and the following year began broadcasting legally on land from Hilversum 4.

Johnnie Walker remembers the day all the other offshore stations closed:

I couldn't believe the whole government machine and the establishment would be so concerned as to stop something that was not causing any harm to anyone and giving such a great deal of pleasure. I hoped it would go on forever and I wanted to be a part of it.

Right and overleaf: On a cold, wet Monday 14 August 1967, DJs Johnnie Walker and Robbie Dale stepped from the London train at Ipswich on their way to Felixstowe and the tender that would take them to Radio Caroline. At midnight, they would be operating outside the law by broadcasting from Radio Caroline. A group of young fans, mostly teenage girls, were there to see them off.

Radio Caroline North and South continued broadcasting programmes to Britain and the Continent for the remainder of 1967. They were there until the ships were silenced on 3 March 1968. It was alleged that the Wijsmuller Salvage Company was owed £30,000 by Radio Caroline, so they eventually took the law into their own hands. They boarded both ships before the day's broadcasting began and seized control. *Caroline* and *Mi Amigo* were towed to Amsterdam by the Wijsmuller Salvage Company, where they remained impounded.

For the many listeners, there was no jovial disc jockeys, no music, just … silence.

Right: All alone. The offshore pirate radio stations closed down on 14 August 1967, except for Radio Caroline, which continued to broadcast from the *Mi Amigo* off Frinton-on-Sea, Essex, and the MV *Caroline* in Ramsey Bay, Isle of Man.

Left: The two Radio Caroline ships in Amsterdam in 1968. On 3 March 1968, the Dutch shipping and salvage company Wijsmuller towed away both Caroline ships to Holland. Wijsmuller had been tendering the ships and supplying crews, but after failing to receive payment took the ships to Amsterdam to sell them and recover outstanding payments. (*Photograph by Alf Smith*)

The 1970s decade of offshore pirates began on 23 January 1970, when the psychedelic-coloured ship MV *MEBO II* began to broadcast the programmes of Radio Northsea International. The station was the brainchild of Edwin Bollier and Erwin Meister, two Swiss engineer millionaires, who wanted to begin their own pirate radio station. They purchased a 347-ton ship, *The Bjarkoy*, built in Norway and renamed it *MEBO* – the first two letters of their surnames MEister and BOllier. Some believed it was named after the Marine Etc., Broadcasting (Offences) Act. Not so!

The ship was too small, so they purchased another, the 630-ton *Silvretta*, built in 1948 at Slikkerveer, in the Netherlands. Regular programmes began on Radio Northsea International – later known as RNI – on 28 February 1970.

MEBO II sailed for England on 23 March 1970, broadcasting as she travelled, and arrived at Holland-on-Sea, Essex, the following day. The station soon experienced jamming, which was carried out by the Ministry of Posts and Telecommunications. They sent out a high-pitched 800 cycles per second tone from Rochester, Kent. Other frequencies were tried, but on each occasion, the jamming continued.

On 13 June 1970, Radio Caroline made a brief appearance when RNI changed its name for the duration of the general election in Britain. Many people believe that the propaganda transmitted by Caroline did have an effect on the outcome of the results, which went against Harold Wilson's Labour government that had outlawed them in 1967.

DJs urged listeners to vote for the party that supported commercial radio. Broadcasters were Andy Archer, Mark Wesley and Alan West. On land, a Caroline bus with Ronan O'Rahilly and Simon Dee aboard toured key marginal seats. The Conservative Party won the election, with Edward Heath taking over from Harold Wilson. What sway Radio Caroline had can never be accurately quantified.

With a win for the Conservative party, commercial radio was assured of a future. Legalised independent radio began in London with LBC on 8 October 1973.

MEBO II reverted to RNI, but the jamming continued. Eventually, the station admitted defeat. On 23 July 1970, the *MEBO II* departed from the Essex coast and returned to Holland, where she resumed broadcasting. However, Meister and Bollier ran out of money and, on 24 September, Radio Veronica paid them to shut up shop … or should that be ship?

As with the majority of offshore stations, they were not off the air for long. Regular programmes began again on 20 February 1971. The station theme 'Man of Action' by the Les Reed Orchestra, was followed by Alan West and the Gilbert O'Sullivan record 'Nothing Rhymed'. The DJs on board were Stevie Merike, Alan West, Tony Allan, Martin Kayne, Dave Rogers and Crispian St John. However, bad news was just around the corner – again!

On the morning of 15 May 1971, three men climbed into a rubber dinghy, left Scheveningen and headed for the *MEBO II*. It took them three hours to reach the ship, but it was not a social visit. Two of the men climbed aboard and went down to the engine room, lit a fire, returned to the dinghy and set sail for the Dutch coast. No one on board the *MEBO II* noticed any visitors.

Within minutes, there was a huge explosion, which started a fire at the stern of the ship. DJ Alan West announced over the radio 'Mayday Mayday! This is the radio ship *MEBO II* 4 miles off the coast of Holland … we require assistance urgently due to a fire on board this vessel caused by a bomb being thrown into our engine room … Mayday Mayday! This is an SOS from Radio Northsea International.' Captain Harteveld, the master of the ship, repeated the SOS in Dutch.

By midnight, the entire stern of the ship was ablaze, and those on board were hoping they would be rescued.

In the early hours of 16 May, the tug, *Eurotrip*, rescued ten men from the *MEBO II*. Shortly afterwards, she was joined by a firefighting tug, *Volans*. Also on the scene was the Dutch Royal Navy frigate, *Gelderland*. The captain of the *MEBO II*, together with the transmitter engineer and ship's engineer, remained on board. The fire raged for another two hours before it was brought under control by a number of ships. Fortunately, neither the radio studio nor the transmitter was damaged, and transmissions recommenced the following day.

Dutch police immediately began an investigation, and within hours three men were arrested after parts of a rubber dinghy and frogmen's suits were found on a deserted beach near The Hague. Each had been paid £3,000 to do the job. Together with Radio Veronica's sales manager, Norbert Jurgens, and a director, 'Bull' Verweij, they appeared in court at The Hague on 20 May 1971. The prosecutor said that Radio Veronica had financed the raid on *MEBO II*, and the men were paid £10,000 to bring the ship inside Dutch waters. They had intended to tow her into port without damage. Veronica had not ordered the fire as they had no wish to endanger life. On 21 September 1971, 'Bull' Hendrik Verweij, Norbert Jurgens and the three divers were found guilty of the attack on the *MEBO II*, and each of the five were sentenced to one year in prison.

On 30 August 1974, RNI agreed to close down. The final English programme was transmitted from 11 p.m. to midnight, when Don Allen, Robin Banks, Roger Kent, Brian McKenzie and Bob Noakes said their farewells. RNI closed down at midnight when the Dutch Marine Offences Act came into force.

The disc jockeys were taken aboard the *MEBO I* and received a hero's welcome when they arrived on land. Engineers remained on board a further week, and the *MEBO II* ship sailed to Rotterdam. Customs sealed up certain sections of the ship. She then sailed on the canals to Slikkerveer. The vessel was then stripped, transmitters serviced and the studios rebuilt.

In future, the ship would be known as RNI – Radio Nova International, and was to be anchored in the Gulf of Genoa by mid-October 1974. It would broadcast in Italian during the daytime and English in the evening. The new station was in honour of the Royal Park Hotel in Zurich, Switzerland, owned by Edwin Bollier.

However, all this turned out to be a dream as the *MEBO II* was impounded by the Dutch police on 10 October 1974 due to the fact the vessel had radio transmitters on board. At a court hearing on 10 December, Edwin Bollier was found guilty of operating a pirate radio ship, and the court ordered that the transmitters should be confiscated. Bollier challenged the Dutch authorities, alleging that they were illegally detaining a Panamanian ship. The transmitters were in the ship's hold and so were technically cargo. Two hearings were held on 3 and 25 March 1975, and the decision was that after a deposit of 250,000 guilders had been paid, *MEBO II* would be free to sail. The money would be returned after two years, providing that the ship did not broadcast to Northern Europe during that time.

More infighting went on between the owners of *MEBO II* and the Dutch. The outcome was that, on 2 January 1976, the company who owned *MEBO II* had to pay a 5,000 guilders fine, after which the ship was free to leave Holland. Rumours were rife that Edwin Bollier had sold the ship to an African company, and so RNI would not be broadcasting to Italy.

On 14 January 1977, it was confirmed that *MEBO II* had been sold to the Libyans for an estimated 6 million guilders. There was also an extra transmitter installed on the ship near the RNI transmitters. It was a Continental Electronics 10 kW transmitter formerly used by Radio Veronica, which had been sold to Meister and Bollier in 1976.

The ship sailed from De Groot & van Vliet Shipyard, Holland, together with her companion ship, the *Angela*. They arrived in Tripoli harbour on St Valentine's Day 1977. The Attorney General at the Court of Justice in The Hague declared that the confiscation of the *MEBO II* had been cancelled, and that she, together with the *Angela* and with the existing transmitting apparatus on board, could leave the Netherlands with due observation of the customs control.

On 2 May 1977, test transmissions began from the *MEBO II* in Tripoli harbour. The *MEBO II* and *Angela* sailed for Benghazi on 8 August, arriving on 11 August. The ships then moved on to Dema harbour, 600 miles east of Tripoli, where the radio ship became known as the Libyan Post-Revolution Broadcasting Station. By 30 October 1977, *MEBO II* was on her way back to Benghazi. She arrived in Tripoli harbour on 19 January 1978.

On 5 April 1978, an article in *Monitor Magazine* reported that *MEBO II* had been purchased by the Libyan government and her name changed to *El Fatah*. The first MEBO, later renamed the *Angela*, became Libyan property at the same time. She then became the *Almasira*.

After six months in harbour, the transmitters were taken off the ship and rebuilt in Libya. The Libyan government had ordered a number of transmitters for land-based stations, but by April 1978 these were not ready, so the former RNI ship was used as a stopgap. Readings from the Holy Koran were regularly broadcast.

Once the transmitters for the land-based stations had been completed, broadcasts from the radio ship ceased. By 1980, she had been stripped of all her broadcasting equipment, used as a target by the Libyan Air Force and sunk. A sad ending to a ship that had enjoyed a colourful existence on the high seas.

Left: The *MEBO II* off the Essex coast in 1970. In June 1970, Radio Caroline took over the transmitters of Radio Northsea International, broadcasting off the Essex coast and urging listeners to vote for the Conservative party, which supported commercial radio. The Labour government's Postmaster General, John Stonehouse, authorised the jamming of the signal with a powerful transmitter near Southend. This was the only time Britain has attempted to jam a radio station. Even during the Second World War, Nazi propaganda broadcasts were not jammed. A Caroline bus, with Ronan O'Rahilly and Simon Dee on board, toured key marginal seats. Ronan O'Rahilly was threatened with years of imprisonment for major infringement of the Representation of the People Act. The legal threats died away after the Conservative Party won the election. There was no way of measuring what effect the station had, if any, on the first time, eighteen-year-old voters. It was the first election in which the voting age had been lowered from twenty-one to eighteen. There was a swing of 1.5 per cent to 2 per cent in marginal constituencies, most in the South East of the country and around London. Ernle Money took the Ipswich seat from Labour for the Conservatives by just thirteen votes.

Radio Caroline Returns as Radio 199

In May 1972, the two Caroline ships were sold at auction by the Wijsmuller company. *Caroline* was sold for scrap, while *Mi Amigo* lived to see another day and was sold for £7,400.

We had to wait until December 1972 for the *Mi Amigo* to broadcast again, under the name Radio 199. A Christmas present for listeners occurred when Radio Caroline reappeared. It was a little confusing as to who was broadcasting, and from which ship. Radio Atlantis appeared aboard the *Mi Amigo* from July 1973. This was a Flemish station. Radio Seagull also broadcast from the *Mi Amigo* in July 1973.

Radio Atlantis

This station was founded by Adriaan Van Landschoot, a wealthy Belgian businessman. He reached a deal with Radio Caroline to transmit programmes from the *Mi Amigo* in Flemish. Transmissions began on 15 July 1973 for three months, until the mast of the *Mi Amigo*, anchored off Scheveningen, collapsed on 1 October 1973.

Transmissions then came from the *Jeanine* from 7 January 1974. The station broadcast a mixture of Flemish and English language programmes. The international service of Radio Atlantis, broadcast in English, and was popular in Belgium.

Radio Atlantis closed on 31 August 1974 due to the Dutch Marine Offences Act.

Radio Mi Amigo

With the departure of Radio Atlantis, Caroline was looking for more income. It came in the form of a proposition to run a station from aboard the *Mi Amigo* (as did Radio Atlantis). Sylvain Tack ran the successful Belgian waffle maker and he met with Ronan O'Rahilly requesting to rent the transmitter during daytime hours. Ronan agreed and the station broadcast popular programmes from 1974 to 1978.

However, in 1978, complaints had been received from Radio Mi Amigo's advertisers about continual breakdowns of transmission, and Sylvain Tack brought the DJs back to land.

Some months later, Radio Mi Amigo returned to air from another ship, the *Centricity*. Her name was changed to the *Magdalena*, and she anchored off the Belgian coast. Regular programmes began on 1 July 1979 on 272 metres (1,100 kHz). The *Magdalena* broke her anchor chain on 18 September 1979 and drifted into Dutch territorial waters. A police launch, the *Delfshaven*, went out and arrested the crew, ordering the ship to be towed into harbour. She was taken by the tug *Furie II* to the nearest harbour, Stellendam. On 26 September she was taken to the breakers yard in Ouwerkerk, burned and broken up.

Prosecutions were brought against the Radio Mi Amigo staff and crew. Eighteen people received prison sentences of three months, and fifteen others were each given a one month suspended sentence. Sylvain Tack was given a prison sentence of one year and seven months. He fell foul of the law again in 1981 and went back to prison, this time in France. He was sentenced to five years six months, but was released in March 1986.

Voice of Peace

The station did not broadcast to the United Kingdom or Europe, but was heard along the Middle East coast, from Egypt to Lebanon.

Regular programming began on 26 May 1973 from aboard the 570-ton Dutch freighter, the *Cito*, built in 1940, which was renamed the *Peace*. The majority of programmes were in English, but some were broadcast in French, Hebrew and Arabic. The station was on-air twenty-four hours a day.

Broadcasters came from the UK, Australia, France, Holland, United States of America and New Zealand. The purpose of the radio ship was to bring peace to the Middle East.

On 1 October 1993, the Voice of Peace began her last day of broadcasting from offshore. The Knesset had granted a licence for the station to broadcast from land. The station closed down at 1.56 p.m.

'Loving Awareness' on Radio Caroline

In 1972, Caroline pulled up her anchor and headed for British waters. The station lacked the mass appeal of the 1960s, as there was more competition with ILR stations and Radio 1 in the UK. She adopted an album format to play rock music. This was described as 'narrow casting', but many listeners rejected the format and went elsewhere for their entertainment. According to Paul Harris,

Right: Life on the *Mi Amigo* in the 1970s was tough, with supplies arriving randomly. In this photograph, Peter Chicago is risking his life as he attempts to recover something from the sea. He is being watched by DJs Simon Barrett and Tony Allan. Peter Chicago is a Caroline legend, often keeping the station on the air in very difficult conditions during the 1970s on the *Mi Amigo*, and in the '80s on the *Ross Revenge*.

Above: The *Mi Amigo* in the mid-1970s. The ship was then anchored much further off the Essex coast. The lifeboat featured in the 1960s photographs has been replaced by a single rubber dingy.

Left: The *Mi Amigo* broadcast the programmes of Radio Caroline and Radio Mi Amigo during the 1970s.

author of *When Pirates Ruled the Waves*, he quotes disc jockey Jay Jackson as saying, 'DJs sounded for the most part like stoned hippies on a trip, and often the music would consist of entire album sides. The energy of Caroline in the 1960s had gone.'

DJ Johnny Lewis disagrees:

The '70s era again in my opinion was important with stations like RNI and Caroline. RNI was the Top 40 station, and what it did it did very well, but Radio Caroline from 1974 was very different with the album format. You could hear whole sides of albums, like Mike Oldfield's *Tubular Bells*, and Pink Floyd's *Dark Side Of the Moon*. No other station in Europe was doing this.

In June 1973, Radio Caroline transmitted two programmes from the *Mi Amigo*: Radio Caroline I, a Top 40 station on 389 metres, and Radio Caroline II, an easy listening station on 259 metres. Among the voices heard at this time were Spangles Muldoon, Andy Archer, Steve England, Roger Day and Paul Alexander.

By March 1974, Ronan O'Rahilly introduced the idealistic concept of 'Loving Awareness' to the programming. Ronan said, 'The concept is quite simple. If you inject love into the lives of all those you meet they will love you for it. When we brought Caroline back in 1972 we decided to give it a new dimension.'

Three months later, 40,000 fans attended a Midsummer's Day Radio Caroline Loving Awareness Festival at Stonehenge.

On 31 August 1974, the Netherlands introduced its own Marine Offences Act, which saw the demise of Veronica, RNI and Atlantis. However, Caroline defied the Dutch authorities. No surprise there! Ronan O'Rahilly expected the Dutch to send in the 'heavy brigade' to silence the ship, so he requested that the *Mi Amigo* sail to international waters off Frinton-on-Sea, the original home of the ship in the 1960s.

She anchored in Knock Deep. Radio Caroline closed its office in the Netherlands, and the administration was run from Playa de Aro, Spain.

DJ Fined for Being a Pirate

In September 1975, Andy Archer was the first British disc jockey to be prosecuted under the Marine Offences Act for being a pirate disc jockey, broadcasting on Radio Caroline. He appeared before the Southend Magistrates Court, was found guilty, and fined £100 with £50 costs.

Speaking in March 2014, Andy said, 'It was all rather exciting at the time. In fact, I felt rather proud to be the first disc jockey to fall foul of the Marine Offences Act.'

Police Board Radio Caroline

On 14 November 1975, twenty uniformed police and Home Office representatives from the Radio Regularity Department boarded the *Mi Amigo*, and arrested two DJs, Simon Barrett and Mike Lloyd, the Dutch captain Werner de Zwart and engineer Peter Chicago. All were handcuffed and taken by police launch, then by patrol car to Southend police station. They were interrogated and locked in a cell. They later appeared before magistrates, and three were found guilty of various sections of the Marine Offences Act, 1967. Barrett was fined £200 with

£50 costs, Lloyd was fined £50 with £25 costs and de Zwart was fined £100 with £50 costs. Chicago had pleaded not guilty and was released on £1,000 bail. He made a further appearance at Southend Magistrates Court on 21 February 1976, was found guilty of repairing and maintaining illicit radio equipment, and fined £100 with £50 costs.

It seemed the flavour of the time that DJs and others were being hauled before the courts. Many more were to follow throughout 1976 and 1977.

More Prosecutions

The police in Liverpool went further. In April 1976, they prosecuted three car owners of displaying a Radio Caroline sticker on their vehicles in the city. A case of 'getting your stickers in a twist'. One of those who appeared at Liverpool Crown Court, John Jackson-Hunter, wore a Caroline T-shirt with skull and crossbones printed on the front. He was sentenced to ninety days imprisonment and fined £500. After forty days, having spent Christmas in prison, he was released from Walton Prison.

In Liverpool, they arrested two men who had put up an advertisement in a cinema foyer promoting a Radio Caroline road show. They were fined £25 with £50 costs.

Capital Radio

Broadcasting from the ship *King David*, regular broadcasts of Capital Radio began on 11 September 1970 in English and Dutch. On 10 November 1970, she lost her anchor and began drifting. A mayday distress signal was broadcast and picked up by Scheveningen Radio. The IJmuiden lifeboat was launched, together with the Noordwijk beach rescue boat. The crew of the *King David* were rescued, with the exception of the captain and electronics engineer who remained on board. The *King David* continued to drift and she ended up on the beach at Noordwijk.

The ship was freed by the tug *Hector* and towed into IJmuiden Harbour and moved to the dry dock at Westerdock in Amsterdam one week later.

On 26 November, police and harbour authorities boarded the *King David*, served notice of the ship's arrest and chained up the wheel.

The operators of Capital Radio, International Broadcasters' Society, was officially declared bankrupt on 24 May 1971, and that was the last we heard of the radio station.

Radio Condor

This station planned to go on-air in 1973, but awaited news of the Dutch Marine Offences Act. A ship was purchased and programmes would be broadcast from aboard the 403-ton ex-Icelantic trawler, *Emma IM 15*.

Radio Condor would go on-air from 9 a.m. to 5 p.m. daily, off Zandvoort, Holland. There would be no commercials, and programmes would be of religious and humanitarian interest, interspersed with 'happy' music. The station implied that they would not be breaking the law as they were not broadcasting advertisements.

The station was beset with problems. On 11 August 1973, the anchor chain broke and the vessel was towed into IJmuiden. The company ran out of money and the only broadcasts from Radio Condor were test transmissions in early August 1974.

Radio Delmare

Programmes began on 21 August 1978 on 192 metres, 1,568 kHz from aboard the 195-ton *Aegir II* anchored at Zeeuws Vlaanderen, near the Dutch/Belgian border, 12 miles off Cadzand.

On 11 September, a Force 9 gale resulted in the *Aegir II* drifting out of control. A number of distress calls were broadcast and the *Smitsbank* took the ship under tow to Rotterdam Harbour. All on board were arrested by the Dutch authorities and appeared in court. However, after a six-hour interrogation by the Rotterdam River Police, and the monitoring service of the Dutch Post Office, they were released, but the authorities called for *Aegir II* to be confiscated, together with the transmitting equipment.

Two more replacement ships, the *Epivan* and *Martina*, were purchased, but Radio Delmare closed its station on 28 September 1979.

Radio Seagull

The station began broadcasting from the *Mi Amigo* on 22 July 1973, but suffered from gales that lasted for over a month in November and December 1973 when the mast collapsed. Described as 'progressive', the station returned to the air on 7 January 1974. However, Radio Seagull suddenly ceased broadcasting on 23 February 1974 and was replaced by Radio Caroline.

Radio Veronica

Programmes began from the *Borkum Riff*, anchored in international waters off Katwijk aan Zee, Holland, on 6 May 1960. The station became very popular with the young people of the Netherlands. The programme format had changed in 1965 from easy listening to Top 40 pop music during the daytime, with specialist shows broadcast in the evening.

One year earlier, the *Borkum Riff* had been towed into harbour and broken up. The former lightship was replaced by a converted trawler, the *Norderney*, which was described as large and luxurious.

On 28 June 1973, the Dutch Chamber of Deputies voted ninety-five to thirty-seven in favour of outlawing the pirate radio stations off the Dutch coast, namely Veronica and RNI. The Act would become effective from 1 September 1974.

On 31 August 1974, Radio Veronica said it would not defy the Dutch Marine Offences Act and would close down that evening at 6 p.m. Disc jockey Rob Out made the final announcement: 'This is the end of Veronica. It is a pity for you, for Veronica and especially for democracy in Holland.' Then followed the Dutch national anthem and the transmitter went silent.

Radio Veronica is now a land-based radio station, operated by Veronica Omroep Organisatie. It has over 1 million members and is one of the biggest broadcasting societies in the Dutch public broadcasting sector.

Left: The *Mi Amigo* off the Essex coast in 1975. It was 29 August 1974 that the ship was towed from off Scheveningen and dropped anchor 18 miles off the Essex coast, close to the Kentish Knock lightship.

The 134-foot transmitting mast, the last to be built on the ship, survived for another six years after the ship sunk in March 1980. It finally fell into the sea in 1986.

Chapter 3
THE EIGHTIES

Tune

Volume

Mi Amigo Sinks

During the night of 20 March 1980, the *Mi Amigo* sank in 25 feet of water. Huge waves finished off the station's fifty-five-year-old vessel, where government legislation had failed.

The ship went down in raging seas just a few miles from Walton-on-the-Naze. She came to rest on Long Sandbank, with 134 feet of her aerial mast showing above the waterline, and pointing directly and defiantly towards the sky. This mast stood above the waves for six years, before finally collapsing into the sea in April 1986. However, this was not the end of the Radio Caroline story.

Radio Caroline Returns on a New Ship

After three years of rumour and speculation, the station returned once again. This time aboard a former 1960-built Icelandic converted trawler, called the *Ross Revenge*. She was the largest ship ever in offshore history, and weighed 978 tons. The ship had a 300-foot high aerial mast. She anchored off the English coast in the Knock Deep, just a mile from where the *Mi Amigo* anchored.

Regular programmes began on 19 August 1983. On 10 June 1987, the *Ross Revenge* pulled up her anchor and sailed out of the Knock Deep to a new position close to South Falls Head, approximately 14 miles north-west of Margate. The decision to sail her to this location was caused by the forthcoming Territorial Sea Act, which would extend British territorial waters from 3 to 12 miles.

On 18 November 1983, seven people were arrested, and later released, by Suffolk police in a swoop against Radio Caroline. Boat owner Mick East, from Melton, Suffolk, said he had brought Andy Archer and three other Caroline staff from

the *Ross Revenge* to Ipswich. When the launch docked, fifteen police officers were waiting. They took the DJs and crew into custody at Ipswich police station, where they were questioned.

Police confirmed the raid, carried out with the assistance of customs officers, and said a report on the matter had been sent to the Director of Public Prosecutions. The DJs had been arrested as illegal immigrants, and Mick East for aiding and abetting illegal immigrants. Sniffer dogs were also used when the launch was searched.

Andy, the first disc jockey to be fined for broadcasting from an offshore radio ship, was unlucky for a second time. He appeared before magistrates at Woodbridge in July 1984, where it was stated that Archer was discovered by police hiding in the fuel tank room of a launch on her return to Suffolk from the Radio Caroline ship. He had been promised a lot of money to go back to Caroline, but he had not been paid since September 1983. Police suspected he was an illegal immigrant. He was prosecuted for broadcasting aboard the *Ross Revenge*. He pleaded guilty and was fined £500 with £100 costs.

Other prosecutions took place throughout the 1980s at Southend Magistrates Court, involving people ferrying supplies to the *Ross Revenge*. All were found guilty and fined.

On 20 January 1984, the *Ross Revenge* ran aground on a sandbank 2 miles inside British territorial waters. The transmitters were switched off and, two days later, the ship was able to return south to her anchorage in the Knock Deep.

Left: The *Mi Amigo* sunk in a storm on 20 March 1980, on the edge of the Long Sands in the Thames Estuary. The mast survived for several years before falling.

At Easter time 1984, Caroline celebrated its twentieth anniversary. A Top 500, compiled from listeners' choices, was broadcast over several days. The No. 1 record was 'Imagine', by John Lennon.

By autumn 1984, Caroline was experiencing financial problems and the DJs were not being paid regularly. Many went unpaid, others badly underpaid. Eventually, a number of DJs left to find alternative work with land-based stations in Independent Local Radio and BBC.

Personal Memories from a Disc Jockey

One of the DJs who joined Radio Caroline in 1986 was Shaun Tilley. He had been offered a job and was given detailed instructions on how to reach the *Ross Revenge* ship. Meeting the author at a social radio gathering in London in 2014, Shaun related:

> It was in a pub in Strood, Kent, where I first met members of the Caroline 'circle of trust'. That evening, after a few pints, we all slept on the floor of a scabby boat kept in Hoo for a couple of hours before being woken at 2 a.m. to make the journey to Ramsgate, where we would board the tender that would finally take us out to the *Ross Revenge* radio ship.
>
> The tender wasn't really a problem for me though, and after what seemed like an entire day, the sight of the *Ross* in the distance

Right: The *Ross Revenge* in 1983.

Above: The two skippers who brought the *Ross Revenge* to the Essex coast, Captain Joe Woods (*left*) and Martin Eve, with a chart on the bridge in August 1983. (*Photograph East Anglian Daily Times*)

Above right: The galley on the *Ross Revenge* in 1983. (*Photograph East Anglian Daily Times*)

Right: Dave Richard on the air from the *Ross Revenge* in 1984.

Left: Some of the original planned line-up for Caroline's return to the air in August 1983 on the transmitting mast, from left: Tom Anderson, Robin Ross, Dave Simmons (who left before the station came on the air), Tony Gareth and Dixie Peach. (*Photograph East Anglian Daily Times*)

Left: Peter Chicago with one of the transmitters on the *Ross Revenge* in 1983. Peter was a transmitter engineer who occasionally presented programmes. He started working with Radio Northsea International on the *MEBO II* as a transmitter engineer in 1970, and joined Radio Caroline in 1972. He was behind the scenes, keeping the station on the air through most of the 1970s and '80s. (*Photograph East Anglian Daily Times*)

Above: Carol Muszka with one of the two generators on the *Ross Revenge* that provided power for the transmitters.

Right: Andy Archer is the only DJ to have presented shows on Radio Caroline in the 1960s, '70s and the '80s. He was on board the *Mi Amigo* when it was towed away in 1968. He was back on board off the Dutch and English coast in the 1970s, and on the *Ross Revenge* in the 1980s. Andy was also part of the team on Radio Northsea International from the *MEBO II*. This photograph was taken on the deck of the *Ross Revenge* in 1983. (*Photograph East Anglian Daily Times*)

was truly magical and will live with me forever. The leap from the tender to the ship itself was a scary one, particularly for somebody barely 5 foot 8 inches. However, I jumped with much gusto! Once on board, there was a weird sizing up by 'some' of the 'suspicious' English jocks, whilst the Dutch crew were far more welcoming and they were staggeringly generous in the recreational sense too, which made time in between my air shifts pass a whole lot quicker.

The cabin was fine, but the bed mattresses were truly awful and my instinct told me to turn them round in an instant, which just goes to show the naivety of youth, as those before me had long made sure that each side was as filth-ridden as the other. The TV reception was truly lousy most days, but there were lots of videos and a copy of *Quadrophenia*, one of my all time favourite movies, to keep us 'entertained'! Evening meals around the table in the mess room were fun due to the many arguments and personality clashes only further fuelled by alcohol. Evening meals were usually cooked by the Dutch lads, and that was mostly lamb chops and anything else they could cobble together. At breakfast time, you had to fend for yourself, but I could cook a mean fry up. Having said that, you had to check that the sausages didn't have anything nasty burrowing through them first.

The toilet could be pretty horrid and I'm far from squeamish. Sometimes, the person who'd been before you clearly hadn't been able

Left: Caroline DJ Dixie Peach in 1983. Dixie moved from Radio Caroline to Radio 1 in 1984 with his show 'Midnight Runner'.

Right: Stuart Russell in the studio on the *Ross Revenge* in 1984. He later used the name Nigel Harris.

to flush so, at least once, I'd have to fill up a bucket or two to throw down that hell hole until it finally cleared. Cold showers were the norm and one well-known Caroline engineer would constantly tell me there was no hot water, although he (somehow) was always able to enjoy one himself. I managed to rumble him one Sunday morning when I was doing the 'Breakfast Show'. The record library was opposite the studio and the shower room was between the two. No hot water I was told, yet the portholes miraculously used to mist up with hefty condensation after he'd been in there! But that's how it was, you weren't considered a radio star on the ship, and rightly so. You were a member of a working ship's crew in between your radio shows, and that meant you were constantly having to paint different parts of the ship as well as carrying buckets of diesel up and down sludgy staircases many times in the dark!

Shaun said that presenting radio shows was great fun, playing Top 40 hits during the day and album tracks at night. Much as he loved being a part of the great lady's history, he wasn't 'playing' at radio. He was hugely ambitious. He was offered a chance

Left: Tom Anderson was the last voice heard from the *Mi Amigo* in March 1980, when the ship sunk during a storm. Tom was on the *Ross Revenge* when the ship arrived off the Essex coast in 1983 and he presented the first programme from the new ship. The studios were still being built when the converted trawler dropped anchor 8 August 1983. The studios were built behind the ship's bridge.

Right: Blake Williams was one of the team that put Laser on the air from the *Communicator.* Blake was a transmitter engineer as well as a DJ. He later joined Radio Caroline. This photograph was taken in June 1984.

to broadcast on BBC World Service and Radio Luxembourg in the summer of 1988, later Capital Gold, London and BBC Television, and has never looked back, other than to remember those early days in his career.

From my days on board Radio Caroline, my fondest memories of my shipmates would be reserved for Judy Murphy and Chuck Reynolds. But that's probably influenced by the fact I worked with Judy for much longer at Radio Luxembourg, when she was better known as Jodie Scott, and Chuck regenerated into Randall Lee Rose, who I shared the airwaves with at Capital Gold for many years after.

Ross Revenge Raided

On 19 August 1989, the *Ross Revenge* was boarded by representatives of the Dutch government. The DTI were also present, but remained on board their customs cutter *Landward*. Caroline remained on-air, and DJ Nigel Harris made the following announcement over the air:

We have now been boarded by the Dutch authorities. We are in desperate need of help. They are going to shut the station down

Left: Laser DJ Charlie Wolf.

Right: Caroline DJs on the deck of the *Ross Revenge* in June 1984, from left: Brian Allen, Dave Richards, Tom Anderson, Jay Jackson and Blake Williams.

and take us all off. We are in international waters and this is a breach of this vessel's rights to be here and we are desperately pleading for help. We need help now. Caroline 558 will be leaving the air any moment now as the boarding party are finding their way to the transmitter room where they are going to dismantle all the broadcasting gear, take the studio to pieces, dismantle the generators and then incapacitate the ship totally.

Radio Caroline abruptly left the air at seven minutes past one. The boarding party of around thirty armed men included Dutch, British, Belgian and French officials. They removed all the studio equipment, records and tapes and took down the aerial array, but left the towers and the new mast sections awaiting erection.

The two medium wave transmitters had their valves removed before the inside of the cabinets were attacked with sledgehammers, and mountings and other components destroyed. The raid on the *Ross Revenge* was covered by all British news media. ITN news bulletins showed film of the *Ross Revenge*, with the large Dutch tug *Volans* alongside. The customs cutter *Landward* could also be seen. Caroline's founder, Ronan O'Rahilly, was interviewed and denied Dutch claims that they were acting within international law.

> Every captain on every ship all over the world would know they're talking absolute nonsense. If you board a ship in international waters, you're committing an act of piracy. There is no question about that.

Radio Caroline stayed off the air for six weeks. New equipment was sent out to the ship in September 1989. The station resumed broadcasting on 1 October 1989, staying on-air in one form or another until November 1990, ahead of the 1990 Broadcasting Act, which was due to come into force at the start of 1991, bringing in draconian new laws against offshore broadcasters. The *Ross Revenge* remained at sea, and was silent for a year while the owners tried to find a way around the new laws. During storms in November 1991, the *Ross Revenge* broke from her moorings and drifted onto the Goodwin Sands, and the crew were rescued by helicopter on 4 November.

Laser 558

Based aboard the MV *Communicator*, Laser 558 began broadcasting on 24 May 1984. The station, owned and operated by Eurad SA, played non-stop international pop music, and was hugely popular in Britain and northern Europe. The station employed six American DJs (it was illegal for British DJs to work on offshore radio stations), and claimed that they were using supply tenders from Spain and were therefore a legal organisation. Many listeners were none too pleased with Independent Local Radio and the national BBC channels, became loyal listeners to Laser 558.

With its slogan, 'You're never more than a minute away from music', the station claimed audience figures of 5 million listeners, unseen since the heydays of the 1960s on Radios Caroline, London, Scotland and other offshore stations.

On 9 August 1985, the Department of Trade and Industry chartered the *Dioptric Surveyor* to anchor nearby to monitor both Laser 558 and Radio Caroline. This ship was later replaced by the larger *Gardline Tracker*.

Proving they had a sense of humour, the DJs aboard the *Communicator* made references to the DTI vessel, poking fun at the ship and staff, and made a tongue-in-cheek record titled 'I Spy For The DTI' by the Moronic Surveyors.

In addition to being spied on twenty-fours a day, Laser 558 suffered from a lack of advertising and severe storms in the North Sea. In February 1985, the *Communicator* lost one of its aerial masts. The station did return to air the following day with a temporary aerial, but on reduced power. The ship had also lost its main anchor and was in danger of drifting into non-international waters. The station closed on 5 November 1985.

The day after the closure of Laser 558, Radio Caroline changed its frequency from 576 to 558 kHz. After the *Communicator* arrived in Harwich, a temporary prohibition order was served by the Department of Transport, who said the vessel was unsafe. This meant the ship could not leave Harwich until repairs had been undertaken to make her seaworthy once again, and any outstanding debts were paid.

In September 1986, it was announced that the *Communicator* was bought by East Anglian Productions and restoration was completed in Essex.

Right: The MV *Communicator* arrived off the English coast in December 1983. The first broadcasts were made in January 1984, with a giant helium balloon holding the transmitting antenna high above the deck. This system was a failure, and it was not until April 1984, when a more conventional mast was built, that the station came on the air and programming started in May 1984.

Above: David Lee Stone with one of the transmitters on the *Communicator*. David was one of the DJs who sailed from America on the *Communicator*.

Right: A view from the bridge of the abandoned helium tanks for the balloon on the deck of the *Communicator* in 1984.

Left: Rick Harris in the 'on-air' studio of the *Communicator*, the home of Laser 558, in 1984.

Above: DJ Jessie Brandon in the galley of the *Communicator* in 1984.

Above left: DJs Steve Masters (*left*) and Rick Harris relaxing on the *Communicator* in 1984.

Below left: The production studio on the *Communicator* with the ship's captain, Tim Levansaler (*standing left*), and DJs Paul Dean (Paul May on Radio Northsea International) and David Lee Stone (*seated*).

Right: Following weeks of blockade by the Department of Trade and a lack of funds, on 6 November 1985, the *Communicator* sailed into Harwich Harbour escorted by the *Gardline Tracker* (*left*) and the Essex police launch *Alert*. The ship was impounded by the Admiralty Marshall. The ship returned to sea in late 1986 and, on 1 December, started test transmissions as Laser Hot Hits. After losing masts in a storm, the station went off the air in April 1987.

Laser Hot Hits

The *Communicator* was purchased by East Anglian Productions in April 1986, and work was undertaken to repair and refurbish the ship to satisfy the Department of Trade and Industry.

Regular broadcasts from Laser Hot Hits began on 7 December 1986. The DJs were all American, and some had also appeared on Laser 558. The station closed on Easter Monday, 20 April 1987.

The station suffered from a succession of technical problems throughout its short life. In addition, Laser Hot Hits experienced a lack of advertising revenue.

The new Territorial Sea Act was introduced on 1 October 1987, which extended the 3-mile limit to 12 miles.

On 3 February 1988, the *Communicator*, which had remained silent at sea, sailed into Harwich and was declared unseaworthy by the authorities. She did survive again as a radio ship in 2004. A number of licensed stations broadcast from the *Communicator* in Scotland and Holland.

Radio Monique

Radio Monique was an offshore station broadcasting to the Netherlands and Belgium. It began transmissions on

Left: On the deck of the *Communicator* in 1984 (from the left) Paul Dean, David Lee Stone, Rick Harris and Michael Dean (cook).

15 December 1984 from the *Ross Revenge*, off the Essex coast. The station had done a deal with Ronan O'Rahilly to rent airtime on 963kHz. Radio Caroline had been broadcasting from the *Ross Revenge* since August 1983, but it failed to bring in enough advertising revenue to continue its operation alone. Management for Radio Monique included Fred Bolland and Mike Mourkens.

In Amsterdam, the judiciary was keen to have the station closed down, and spoke with British authorities to ban all activities from the offshore stations transmitting off the English coast.

The authorities did not have to wait too long.

Monique was sold in October 1987, but continued broadcasting from the *Ross Revenge*. However, one month later, the aerial mast on the ship broke during a storm and Radio Monique ceased broadcasting on 24 November 1987.

On 9 July 1988, another station, Radio 558 (later Radio 819 from 5 November), began broadcasting Dutch language programmes from the *Ross Revenge*. Many believed this to be a successor to Monique, as it was similar in format playing pop music, Top 40 songs and featuring Dutch artists, with disc jockeys and advertisers who had been heard on Monique. The station ceased broadcasting on 19 August 1989 when the ship was raided.

Right: Ray Anderson with the radio ship *Communicator* in Harwich Harbour, soon before putting Laser Hot Hits on the air in 1986.

The *Ross Revenge*, home to Radio Monique.

By 1990, Radio Caroline was the sole remaining pirate station at sea. The Marine Offences Act of 1967 in the UK, and 1974 in the Netherlands, sought to make pirate radio difficult and unprofitable, but not impossible. Even with the Act in force, Caroline continued and was joined at times by Radio Northsea International and Laser 558.

Offshore radio, the correct description for those who broadcast from ships and forts, is commonly referred to as 'pirate radio'. Pirate radio on land was not covered by this law, but by much earlier legislation – the 1947 Wireless Telegraphy Act. The original land pirates, all using AM, tended to be idealists, broadcasting in protest against the Marine Offences Act and were, at first, easy to track down and close. The station operators were mostly accepting of this and compliant.

Broadcasting Act 1990 and Wireless Telegraphy Act 2006, Amended 2007

A new act, the 1990 Broadcasting Act, deregulated radio and allowed for three new national stations, as well as many regional, local and also small-scale community stations. However, the increasing effect of deregulation was that commercial stations, previously independent within the areas they covered, could now be bought out and absorbed in to larger groups. The result today is that while there are many stations, most are owned by a few major operators and their output is networked and identical. A small part of the same act awarded the government draconian powers to act against Radio Caroline, with the option to use the military and any degree of force, while providing immunity from counter prosecution for persons acting against the station, even in international waters.

It was believed that the possession of a genuine broadcast licence from a foreign state might protect Caroline from these new clauses, and such a licence was sought. But before significant progress could be made, the station's ship, *Ross Revenge*, was shipwrecked on the Goodwin Sands and brought in to Dover in a complete but derelict condition, and impounded by the UK authorities.

On land, the spread of FM made pirate radio technically more difficult to act against. A respected and responsible land pirate, Radio Jackie, had identified that, contrary to opinion, those tracing and closing these stations – first the General Post Office and later the Radio Investigation Service – did not actually have permission to confiscate broadcast equipment. For a while, this led to some stations being unhindered for long periods, but this loophole was closed when the Wireless Telegraphy Act was amended in early 2007. Land-based pirates still proliferated, especially when technology enabled the studio to be placed remotely from the transmitter and aerial. Many pirates also use the internet legally and profess to have no connection with the broadcast being relayed on FM. Further, now that the activity is run for profit, investigators may encounter violence and risk.

Raids take place with consideration being given to the power of the unlicensed transmitter, the content of the broadcast and the degree of interference caused and the possibility of resistance. Penalties for unlicensed broadcasting allow a fine of up to £2,000 and/or three months imprisonment. It was considered that there were 500 pirate stations operating in the UK by 1990, and certainly no less today. An Ofcom survey for London concluded that the public listened to pirates since commercial radio and the BBC failed to cater for their needs, such as the desire to hear new music.

A Land-Based Pirate

Another 'responsible' pirate, and the first to eventually gain a licence, was Gordon Mac, known as the Godfather of Dance Music, who was a land-based pirate. He ran Sound City in 1983, but the station was closed down by the authorities. Not one to give in easily, he set up a new station, Kiss FM, on 7 October 1985. By 1987, Kiss FM had become London's second-most popular station, with an audience of some 500,000 listeners. Mac was the first person to succeed in taking a pirate radio station to legislation in the UK. By December 1989, Kiss FM was granted a legal licence to become the UK's first black music radio station.

I met up with Gordon in 2012:

We were land-based pirates and had an engineer who set up a microwave so we could broadcast from anywhere in London. This microwave link was aimed at a tower block somewhere in the city with a transmitter located on the roof. It was very hard for the DTI to locate the studio from where we broadcast, but I have to admit we lost hundreds, and I mean hundreds, of transmitters.

The DTI had antiquated laws that said nobody could broadcast illegally as we could be spies. It was only when deregulation was introduced in the 1990s that we managed to progress with stations that legally broadcast specialist music, that continued to this day.

Kiss FM was set up as pirate station specifically to reflect the new dance culture among young people. In December 1989, we won an Independent Local Radio licence to broadcast Kiss FM legally in London. The station was launched in September 1990.

Caroline Continues Broadcasting

Soon after the shipwreck in 1991, Caroline negotiated to reoccupy the ship and also agreed to pay the salvage costs, albeit in small installments. Plans were then made to broadcast for the first time on FM by paying for a twenty-eight-day licence. The studios on board *Ross Revenge,* within Granville Dock, were used, but the transmitter was on top of Dover Castle at a height that gave reception in France.

After many repairs, including reinstalling all the items taken when the ship was raided at sea, *Ross Revenge* was able to leave Dover under tow by the tug *Sea Challenge,* and was taken to the River Blackwater in Essex. More short-term broadcasts were made at places such as Bradwell, Clacton, Southend, London Docklands, the River Medway and finally Tilbury, Essex.

The station also used SW transmissions from the USA, Ireland and Latvia, analogue and digital satellite and, most recently, internet webcasting and phone apps.

Talking to the author in June 2014, Peter Moore relates,

I did some work for Caroline in the seventies and became more involved from 1985. I wanted to be close to a subject that interested me and to have some fun. It was never my intention to get deeply or centrally involved, but circumstances outside

Right: The *Ross Revenge* in 1994. During the early '90s, the ship was detained in Dover harbour and later taken to the River Blackwater, Essex, where this photograph was taken off Bradwell in 1994. The two masts were built at sea to replace the massive mast, which fell into the sea in November 1987.

my control caused that to happen. After being shipwrecked, we found ourselves with a ruined boat, no money and no broadcasts. The options were to give up or find a new direction.

Remaining staff agreed to work for no wages and a small band of supporters offered regular donations, and in this way we started all over again.

It was possible to make legal short-term broadcasts with a very small range, so we broadcast to Dover as a gesture to show that Caroline still existed.

There was no way to get a sizeable audience, but there was the novelty that, for the first time, people could both listen to and visit something that hitherto had been invisible.

With varying degrees of success, we made further similar broadcasts until starting to experiment with satellite radio, first part time and then full time. The change from analogue to digital made this affordable. This gave international range and high quality, but always hampered by the fact that the public use satellite to view television and not to listen so much to radio.

Right: Johnny Lewis worked on Caroline in the 1970s as both broadcaster and engineer, until the *Mi Amigo* sank in 1980. He later worked for the Voice Of Peace and Laser 558, before rejoining Caroline on the *Ross Revenge*. He has also worked for a clutch of Irish stations, as well as local commercial radio in the UK. He now presents shows on Radio Caroline's online service, www.radiocaroline.co.uk.

Left: DJ Pandora in the digital studio on the *Ross Revenge* in 2004. This area was used by Radio Monique in the 1980s, and is featured in the photograph of Tom Anderson on page 90.

We used internet radio, starting at a time when this was considered to be unreliable and expensive for the listener, but watched over time, it became mainstream and of course is global. With this and the possibility of mobile listening by phone apps, we gave up satellite in 2013 as it was by then old technology.

A plan was made to send a second service of Caroline playing a different style of music, but presently we have decided to send a second stream adjusted to American time, where we have a growing following and then maybe a third timed stream for Asia.

Of course, we have our ship, now substantially rebuilt and converted for the sole purpose of transmitting on AM. Four years ago, we asked the UK regulator Ofcom for one AM frequency for our use. The response was that this simply was not possible, but later that such may be possible at some future date and under certain circumstances. But even with the support of our listeners and over seventy British MPs, who put Ofcom under some pressure, we seem no nearer to our goal. British bureaucracy, especially when enjoying a monopoly, sees no urgency, is risk averse and is so mired in rules, that no decisive action is possible. But we will keep repeating our request.

I hope that my work is in part responsible for the fact that Caroline survived and is now stable and experiencing steady expansion, but it is more due to the loyalty and generosity of our supporters and the charisma of the Caroline name. For these reasons I am sure the station will continue for years to come.

Many people believe that the offshore radio stations of the 1960s are responsible for much of the format established by the BBC and commercial radio. DJs aboard the ships and on forts were popular, and in some cases as popular as the artists they played. The stations commanded huge audiences. Today, however, the musical scene has changed.

Johnny Lewis served on various ships in the offshore days and still continued to broadcast for Radio Caroline on land. Attending Radio Day 2014, in Amsterdam, he related:

I think one way or another there is always going to be a place for Radio Caroline. The station's sound has evolved again and we mix new and old album tracks with a very relaxed presentation style. The station also has a very extensive music library and uses it unlike some stations. The presenters are very passionate about the music and the station, and this comes across. The station is still unique in the fact it still has a radio ship and we do use it from time to time, as well as land studios.

I was lucky to learn my trade with some very good broadcasters. On a ship we lived, breathed and talked radio, music and life skills twenty-four hours a day. What made the offshore stations so good and popular, in my view, was we all worked as a family and team.

Right: The Radio Caroline record library on board the *Ross Revenge* at Tilbury in 2004.

Tune

Volume

MV *Aegir II* – Radio Delmare

Two ships, *Aegir* and *Aegir II*, were used by Radio Delmare. *Aegir* started her life as a 250-ton trawler, named after the Norse sea god. Built in 1929 in Groningen by Koster shipyard, she was formerly the MV *Express* and later the *Panicopania*. She was 118 feet long and took cargo from Holland to Denmark, Sweden and Germany. Her stay as a radio ship was short-lived, only broadcasting from 21 August to 11 September 1978, when she broke her anchor chain, drifted into Dutch waters and was boarded by police in the harbour of Maassluis. She first went to the Entrepot harbour of Rotterdam, and later went to the breakers yard and was scrapped.

Converting the ship *Aegir II* into a radio station began in the summer of 1978. She was also built in 1929 at the yard of J. Koster in Groningen, Netherlands. She was 138 feet long and weighed 270 tons. Conversion took place in Scheveningen

harbour. By now, the Dutch Marine Offences Act was in force, so it did not take long for the police to swoop on the vessel and confiscate much of the radio equipment.

In *The Times* on 26 June 1978 we read:

Police officers, accompanied by special Post Office investigators, seized radio transmitting equipment on board a coaster lying in the harbour at Scheveningen, near The Hague on Friday night. They also took possession of 10,000 records, 225 magnetic tapes and a complete inventory for two radio studios.

The transmitters were suitable for medium wave, short wave and VHF broadcasts and were capable of providing Europe-wide coverage, police said.

The coaster's master and two technicians who were installing the equipment were detained for questioning by the police and later released.

According to the ship's master, the coaster had been rented by unidentified people who intended to make offshore broadcasts. The master said he had been offered a considerable amount of money once the broadcasts started.

In August 1978, *Aegir II* sailed out to sea anchoring near the Belgian/Dutch border at Zeeuws-Vlaanderen, 12 miles off Cadzand. With new equipment on board, Radio Delmare began transmissions on 21 August 1978 on 1,902 metres, 1,568 kHz.

The *Aegir II* drifted in a Force 9 gale and was taken in tow to Rotterdam harbour. All on board were arrested and brought before the courts. The ship was later moved and chained up in the Maasluis harbour on the order of the Dutch Prosecutor, Mr Pieterse, who called for the confiscation of the ship and also the transmitting equipment.

Two more replacement ships, the *Epivan* and *Martina*, were purchased, but Radio Delmare closed its station on 28 September 1979.

The *Aegir II* was scrapped in 1981 at Zierikzee, the Netherlands.

MV *Borkum Riff* – Radio Veronica

The *Borkum Riff*, an ex-German 450-ton lightship, 141 feet in length, was built in 1911 and located in Emden, West Germany. It was retired from service in 1959 and purchased by Radio Veronica's shareholders for 63,000 guilders to become Europe's first pirate radio station. The ship was rebuilt and refitted as a broadcasting vessel at the Karstens-Werft in Emden in 1959. On 18 April 1960, the *Borkum Riff* left Emden, towed by the British tug *Guardsman* to a location off Katwijk aan Zee. She broadcast as Radio Veronica from 21 April 1960 to 16 November 1965. After the *Norderney* took over as the home for Radio Veronica, the *Borkum Riff* was sold for scrap and broken up in Zeebrugge.

MV *Norderney* – Radio Veronica

The 399-gross ton, 148-foot long and 27-foot wide MV HH 294 *Paul J. Müller* was built in 1949/50 by the Deutsche Werft AG in Finkenwerder, Germany, for the Paul Müller shipping company in Hamburg. The vessel served as a fishing boat in international waters off Iceland. In July 1956, the vessel was sold to the Niedersächsische Hochseefischerei GmbH in Cuxhaven and renamed NC 420 *Norderney*. In 1960, the ship was sold to be scrapped in the Netherlands. In 1964, the three Verweij brothers bought the vessel on behalf of Radio Veronica as a replacement for the *Borkum Riff*.

The ship, a former trawler, was rebuilt at the ZSM Zaanlandse Scheepsbouw Maatschapij shipyard in Zaandam, Netherlands. On 16 November 1964, the Wijsmüller ship *Nestor* towed the *Norderney* to a position off Scheveningen.

The *Norderney* broadcast programmes from Radio Veronica from 16 November 1964 to 31 August 1974. Since 8 December 2013, the *Norderney* has been a restaurant and events boat, permanently moored in Amsterdam in part of the harbour near where the former REM Island is also now a restaurant.

MV *Caroline*, Originally the *Fredericia*

The 763-ton passenger ferry MV *Caroline* was originally named the *Fredericia* and was built by Voerf and Flyedok in 1930 in Frederikshavn, Denmark, on the north-east coast of the Jutland peninsular in northern Denmark. Her length was 188 feet with a beam of 18 feet, and could travel at a speed of 18 knots. The vessel served as a ferry boat on the Baltic until 1963.

Plans had been drawn up for her to be converted into a floating offshore radio station as the MV *Caroline*, and the ship was registered in Panama. She was sold for £20,000 to Cross Channel Container Services Limited of Greenore Harbour, Ireland. The company was owned by Aodhogan O'Rahilly, father of Ronan O'Rahilly. She left Rotterdam for Greenore on 13 February 1964, arriving on 5 March.

A 165-foot mast was erected, a large anchor system was installed and the ship strengthened to withstand continuous assault by gale-force winds and waves. On 26 March, the MV *Caroline* set sail under the command of Dutch Merchant Navy Captain George Baeker. Her destination was given as Spain. A Royal Navy destroyer inspected the MV *Caroline* as she passed Plymouth. On 27 March at 1800 hours, the MV *Caroline* dropped anchor off the coast of Felixstowe, Suffolk.

On 6 May 1964, a government customs launch, *Venturous*, flying the blue ensign, drew alongside. A young officer requested permission to board the MV *Caroline*. Captain Baeker refused permission, saying it was against the law as they were in international waters, but would allow one man to come across in a lifeboat. The offer was not accepted. The *Venturous* turned and sailed away.

On 2 July, Radio Caroline and Radio Atlanta announced that the stations would merge. The MV *Caroline* would anchor off the coast of Ramsey, Isle of Man, and broadcast as Radio Caroline North, while the MV *Mi Amigo* would change ID to Radio Caroline South. Ronan O'Rahilly and Allan Crawford became joint managing directors. On 3 July, the MV *Caroline* set sail under the command of Captain Hengeveld for the Isle of Man and continued to broadcast as she sailed. On 5 July, the ship was off Anglesey, Wales. MV *Caroline* dropped anchor in Ramsay Bay, Isle of Man, at 3.32 p.m. on Monday 6 July 1964. During a severe south-westerly gale on 13 January 1965, the starboard anchor was lost and the ship started to drift. Within a week, a new 1½-ton anchor was fitted, including 4½ tons of chain.

The Marine Offences Act then came into force at midnight on 14 August 1967. The legislation prevented supplies being delivered to any radio ship from British ports. Radio Caroline continued broadcasting, but supplies were delivered from the Netherlands.

In 1968, a dispute arose with the Wijsmuller Company of the Netherlands, who serviced the ship with supplies, who said they were owed around £30,000 for tender services to both Radio Caroline ships.

On 2 March 1968, the powerful Dutch tug *Utrecht* dropped anchor a mile from the MV *Caroline*, but showed no signs of wanting to communicate with the MV *Caroline*. The following morning at 0200 hours, a loud thump was heard. Before anyone could get to the deck, Dutch seamen burst into the lounge. The captain, chief DJ and the chief engineer were summoned to the lounge and a letter was read out from the Wijsmuller tender firm that stated that all broadcasting was to cease, the studios sealed and the transmitters crystals to be removed. After heated discussions, the staff on the MV *Caroline* complied with the order to avoid all possibilities of violence. The crew was left in the dark regarding their future – were they being taken to Greenore to have the unused 50,000 watt transmitter, which was still cased in the hold, installed, or were they returning off the Essex coast? Unknown to the crew, the same events were happening on the MV *Mi Amigo*. One of the Wijsmuller brothers wanted to continue providing this service while the other did not, and had instructed two raiding parties to bring in the Caroline ships. At 1800 hours, the anchor systems were cut away, a towline fixed between the MV *Caroline* and the tug *Utrecht*, and a long, slow tow southwards began. At times, Navy vessels were seen following them. On 9 March, the MV *Caroline* arrived in Amsterdam, the staff were paid and given air tickets back to England and told to wait for instructions, but none came.

On 29 May 1972, the MV *Caroline* was sold at a public auction for £3,117 to Frank Rijsdijk-Holland NV of Hendrick Ido-Ambacht, in the western Netherlands, for demolition. In 1980, the MV *Caroline* was scrapped by shipbuilder and demolition company Van de Marel of Ouwerkerk, Netherlands, and was broken up. Her broadcasting career had run from Good Friday, 27 March 1964, and ended on 2 March 1968.

Right: The MV *Fredericia* sailed to anchor off the Isle of Man as Radio Caroline North.

MV *Cheeta II* – Radio Mercur and Radio Caroline South

In January 1961, the *Cheeta* was replaced by the 450-ton Norwegian coastal ship, which had been called *Habat* and *Mosken*, now renamed *Cheeta II*.

As an offshore radio station, she broadcast as Radio Mercur from 31 January 1961 to 10 July 1962. In the summer of 1962 (after Radio Mercur's broadcasts had stopped), the vessel was called *San Pedrito* for a short period, and was moored in Copenhagen harbour, before moving to Flensburg in Germany. It was later sailed back to a position off Copenhagen, having been sold to Mrs Britt Wadner, who was known in Sweden as the 'Viking Lady' and was a national celebrity. *Cheeta II* then became Radio Syd from 28 September 1964 to 19 January 1966.

On 20 January 1966, thick pack ice forced the *Cheeta II* to leave her anchorage. Following the grounding of the Radio Caroline South ship, she sailed to a position off Frinton-on-Sea, Essex, to take her place while repairs were carried out. She began broadcasting as Caroline South on 13 February 1966 until 1 May 1966.

Radio Caroline disc jockey Colin Nichol was the first to go on board the Swedish ship with Britt Wadner and Ronan O'Rahilly. He recalls:

My first impressions were that she looked a homely kind of ship. She appeared to have been a typical old ferry. We went into the lounge and while I was still grinning with pleasure on finding so much polished wood trimming and panelling aboard, and marvellous glass swing doors to penetrate and explore beyond. Ronan was calling to me in excitement and saying 'Isn't she marvellous – what a great room.'

I returned for a further ten days to help the Swedish personnel on board organise the studio and living quarters for the English DJs. We were hardly ready for the invasion when it happened – after all, the ship was still nowhere near ready to broadcast when, one day, the tender came alongside, loaded to the gunwales with the other Caroline DJs all shouting and waving, and shattering the peaceful interlude we had been enjoying for more than a week past.

More cabins were allotted, sheets and blankets found, and I decided to go ahead with the plan I had at the time just before the *Mi Amigo* went aground. After going ashore on leave shortly after this time, I resigned from Radio Caroline in the hope of working ashore, and believed (wrongly as it turned out) that I'd seen the last of the saga of pirate radio. It was quite some time afterwards that the *Cheeta II* made her presence felt on the airwaves, and became an only partly successful, on-again, off-again, replacement for the *Mi Amigo*.

I will always remember those very happy evenings spent on the *Cheeta II*, with my newfound Swedish friends. Those late suppers, with smorgasbord, huge sandwiches, coffee, and listening to other radio broadcasts from all over the world on the big radio in the lounge.

She's a ghost ship now, in the Gambia River, sunk and useless. But she left a warm place in my heart, and now I understand a sailor's feeling for his ship.

The *Cheeta II* remained at anchor between Radio Caroline and Radio London until 21 July 1966, when she broke anchor and needed assistance from a tug, the *Agama*. She was towed into Harwich Harbour, where she anchored to two buoys in the River Stour off Wrabness.

Ronan O'Rahilly (*right*) with Brit
Wadner and Colin Nichol onboard
the *Cheeta II* in 1966.

The *Cheeta II* in Harwich Harbour in 1966.

A few days later, a warrant of arrest was tied to its mast by the customs authorities in Harwich. The *Cheeta II* remained at anchor for the next five months, On 23 January 1967, a second summons warrant was nailed to its mast. The East Anglian press reported on 27 February 1967 that *Cheeta II* left Harwich the previous day towed by a tug. The writs that had been served on the ship had been lifted. It was believed the ship's destination was Flushing in Holland.

Later, in 1967, the ship headed for Spain and the Canary Islands, and the following year the vessel sailed for Gambia, where she was laid to rest.

Mrs Britt Wadner died Friday 13 March 1987, aged seventy-two years.

MV *Comet* – Radio Scotland

The *Comet* was a former lightship, *LV 001*, that operated off the coast of Ireland. She had been built at John Brown's shipyard on the River Clyde in 1904. Weighing in at 500 tons, she measured 90 feet in length with a beam of 23 feet, built with a steel frame and iron decks at a cost £6,740, for use of Dun Laoghaire, a suburban seaside town in Dublin Bay.

Lightships were to serve the mariner on the Irish coast for 264 years, until the last vessel was withdrawn from its station at South Rock in Co. Down in February 2009.

By the start of the twentieth century, Trinity House light vessels were permanently manned, and had a crew of eleven, seven of whom (a master and six ratings) would be on active duty at any one time. It was an extremely demanding and dangerous profession, and it would take fifteen to twenty years of service to be promoted to master.

Following decommissioning in 1965 by the Commissioner of Irish Lights, she was towed to St Sampson's port in Guernsey to be fitted out as a radio ship to operate off the Scottish coast. Transmitters and studio equipment were supplied by RCA. The owners were keen that the station should launch on Hogmanay 1965, so there was a deadline and considerable pressure on the engineering team. The ship had two diesel engines feeding two 10 kW transmitters, giving a total power of 20 kW. The aerial was an omni-directional folded dipole, 145 feet high.

The station went on-air on New Year's Eve 1965. However, it was touch-and-go if the station would achieve its on-air date and time. Disc jockeys and engineers waited patiently for hours in a hotel in Dunbar, East Lothian. The ship had been expected to arrive at noon the previous day, then at four o'clock. However, bad weather delayed the *Comet*, as she was towed at 4 knots up the east coast from the English Channel to international waters off Fife Ness, about 25 miles east of Edinburgh.

She did arrive in the early hours of New Year's Eve. The technical director, Patrick Hargreaves, said, 'A great deal of technical work requires to be done before we can broadcast. We might just make it.'

The station did go on-air successfully at Hogmanay, as the bells were ringing in the New Year for 1966. The programmes were heard all over Scotland as well as Scandinavia. At night, the signal on 242 metres medium wave could be heard in London. However, in the west of Scotland, there were complaints that the signal was not coming in very strongly. So, in April 1966, the *Comet* completed a 1,000-mile trip around the north of Scotland, but she had no engine so had to be towed. On her journey, she encountered storms and the ship almost caught fire at one stage.

The *Comet* anchored off Troon in the Firth of Clyde, then Ballywater, County Down and, finally, back off the east coast of Scotland to its former location off Dunbar.

In March 1967, the station was prosecuted for broadcasting within territorial waters and fined £80. Radio Scotland ceased transmission immediately, but broadcasting recommenced in April 1967.

Tommy Shields, the managing director, a former publicity executive for Scottish Television, journalist and playwright, said that, by the beginning of August 1967, he and the six directors of the station had lost roughly £100,000. Had the station operated until the end of the year, they would have come 'out of the red'. He said his twenty-two-month campaign to operate a commercial radio station was 'a great adventure', but said it was a shame they had lost the battle. Tommy went on to say,

> Never in my life – and that's been quite a while – has there been such public demonstration of protest as there has been against the decision to ban the pirates. What concerns them is the decision to deprive them of a radio service they have become accustomed to, and want to keep.

Senior disc jockey Ben Healy closed the station on 14 August 1967 just before midnight by saying, 'We have all enjoyed being a pirate team. Life at sea had some drawbacks but was a great experience.'

Tommy Shields never recovered from the decision by the government to close the offshore stations on 14 August 1967. He died just six months later, aged only forty-nine years.

The *Comet* was towed into Methil Docks, Fife, on the afternoon of Friday 18 September 1967, where it was moored for two weeks. Captain Willie Fisher and engineer Jack Johnstone were on board while the ship was stripped of its mast and transmitter equipment before being taken to Flushing harbour, where it was rebuilt into a house ship. Many years later, it went to Van de Marel shipbreakers in Ouwerkerk, where it was broken up.

MV *Communicator* – Laser 730, 558 and Laser Hot Hits, Holland FM and Radio Veronica 1224

The *Communicator* had a number of names before she entered the offshore radio history – the *Tananager*, *Charterer* and *Gardline Seeker*. She was built in 1954 by Abeking and Rasmussen in Lemwerder, Germany, as a cargo vessel operating between Bergen, Stavanger and Oslo. She weighed 490 tons and was 177 feet in length.

In August 1983, the *Gardline Seeker* was sold to Deka Overseas Ltd of Madison Avenue, New York, and she sailed to Port Everglades having been cleaned in dry dock at the Tractor Marine quayside. She left Port Everglades and sailed to New Ross, Ireland, where she was converted into a radio ship and renamed MV *Communicator*. It was registered in Panama.

At the end of December 1983, the ship arrived in international waters off Margate, Kent. She suffered many problems, including an anchor chain breaking, unsuccessful tests with helium balloons, losing one of its aerial masts, generator problems, the ship going adrift and 'Eurosiege'.

DJ Johnny Moss remembers:

Before we started broadcasting, the station was to be called Laser 730. A guy called Blake Williams and myself had to get a signal out of the ship with no radio mast, just using the ships masts, which were not very tall. This was to show the owner we could broadcast from the boat, but needed proper radio towers. The Americans thought they could use a helium balloon holding the aerial. Not a good idea in the North Sea in winter. Blake and myself made this wire aerial and fixed it to both ships masts, we got a signal out, but because the voltages were so high at times the aerial looked more like a firework display. But it did the job, the owner put the cash up for proper radio masts and Laser 558 was born.

On 7 November 1985, the *Communicator* was put under arrest and was moored on the River Stour, off Edwarton Ness (Harwich). Government ship keepers remained on board the MV *Communicator*, keeping guard.

On 21 April 1986, East Anglian Productions put out a press release stating that they had purchased the MV *Communicator* and all the equipment on board for £35,000. On 10 November, a Panamanian official issued the MV *Communicator* its certificate. On 15 November, DTI officials inspected the ship and lifted the detention order. The next day the *Communicator* sailed into international waters, and moored in the Cork anchorage near to Sealand, 15 miles off Felixstowe.

Above right: The MV *Galaxy*, home of Radio London, in an aerial photograph taken in 1965.

Below right: The MV *Communicator* off the Essex coast in June 1984.

Ray Anderson in the
production studio on board the
MV *Communicator*,
22 April 1986.

On 19 May 1987, the MV *Communicator* was towed from off the Essex coast to Fairy Bank, 20 miles off Dunkirk, by a Belgian trawler. The reason for this was the forthcoming Territorial Sea Act, which would extend the British territorial waters from 3 to 12 miles. On 15 August, the ship was moved to the Gabber sandbank, about 15 miles off Harwich and within sight of the MV *Ross Revenge*. On 3 February 1988, the MV *Communicator* sailed back into Harwich Harbour, Parkestone Quay. Two days later, the vessel was moved to Edwarton. Studio equipment was removed from the ship. On 6 February, the MV *Communicator* was moored in a scrapyard at Mistly on the south bank of the River Stour, near Manningtree.

In August 1989, the *Communicator* was towed to Lisbon, Portugal. In July 1993, the *Communicator* was temporarily renamed *Albatross* and sold to Old Court Shipping Corporation of Panama City, Panama. On 3 June 1994, a contract was signed in Portugal between Peparacoes Navais do Jego, LDA, and Holland FM for the sale of the MV *Communicator* for a rumoured sum of $100,000. On 11 August, the *Communicator* was towed by the tug *Vlieland* from Lisbon to IJmuiden. The vessel served as a broadcasting ship for Holland FM, which was taken over by Radio Veronica in 1995.

As the MV *Communicator* the ship broadcast as Laser 730 (January–March 1984); Laser 558 (May 1984–November 1985); Laser Hot Hits 576 (December 1986–April 1987); and Radio Sunk (October 1987). She also broadcast on a number of licenced Dutch stations in 1994 and 1995–2002.

The ship sailed to the Orkney Islands, where she broadcast as a Restricted Service Licence as the Super Station from 4 September to 30 November 2004. The ship was later cut up and sold as scrap.

MV *Galaxy* – Radio London

Formerly the USS *Density*, which was launched 6 February 1944 by Tampa Shipbuilding Co., Inc., Tampa, Florida, USA, and commissioned 15 June 1944. Lieutenant Commander R. R. Forrester Jnr, USNR, was in command. She was reclassified MSF-218, 7 February 1955.

The vessel arrived at San Diego on 23 September 1944 to serve as a training ship for the Small Craft Training Center at Terminal Island, until 2 February 1945, when she sailed for Pearl Harbour and Ulithi. The *Density* sortied from Ulithi on 19 March 1945 to sweep mines, preparatory to the invasion of Okinawa on 1 April. She patrolled off Okinawa for its capture and occupation.

The *Density* remained in the Far East on occupation duty until 20 November, when she sailed for the United States' west coast, arriving at San Diego on 19 December 1945. The *Density* was decommissioned in Galverston, Texas, on 3 March 1947. The ship received three battle stars for her Second World War service.

The *Density* was sold to two Greek brothers in 1960, and for three years was used as a small cargo ship. She was put up for sale once again and, in 1964, was sold for $60,000 to two American businessmen, Don Pierson and Tom Danaher. The ship was converted into a floating radio station at Miami and renamed MV *Galaxy*. Conversion costs came to $500,000 and she was registered in Honduras.

She left Miami on 22 October 1964, and sailed across the Atlantic for British waters and the Essex coast, arriving on 19 November 1964. The station would be known as Radio London – Big L. Regular programming began on 23 December

1964 and became hugely popular within a short space of time, giving Radio Caroline South a run for its money.

The *Galaxy* may have been a heavy ship, but gale-force winds did cause her problems. On 11 January 1966, a Force 8 storm occurred off Walton-on-the-Naze, the ship began to drift and the anchor chain broke. The transmitter was switched off. She drifted to within yards of the Radio Caroline ship, *Mi Amigo*. The Clacton lifeboat was launched, but the *Galaxy* was safe after drifting 4 miles towards Clacton Pier. The following day, the Felixstowe tug *Kent* towed the *Galaxy* back to her original anchorage. Broadcasting began again at 1 p.m.

The Marine Offences Act came into operation at midnight on 14 August 1967. Radio London ceased broadcasting at 3 p.m. that afternoon. The *Galaxy* set sail for Hamburg on 19 August, where she was dry-docked. It was the intention to sell her as a going radio station, but her condition had deteriorated and the idea was aborted. She was eventually sold for scrap in 1970 and moved to Kiel, where she remained for many years as a dive training vessel to practice underwater repair techniques. On 20 April 1979, she sank. Seven years later, she was raised due to concerns about fuel leaks. She was scrapped on dry land.

MV *Jeanine* – Radio Atlantis 1973/74

The *Jeanine* began life as the 403-ton Icelandic trawler, *Emma* IM15, and was built by de Dollard shipyard, Landsmeer, Holland, in 1956. During April 1964, the *Emma* was chartered by an oil company for drilling exercises in the North Sea. In 1967, the vessel was owned by NV Marezaten, and was sold to the Ouwehands fishing company in Katwijk aan Zee, Holland. They renamed the ship *Zeeland* KW122. In 1970, the ship was decommissioned from herring fishing and tied up in Katwijk harbour.

Three years later, the ship was sold as scrap to Steph Willemsen for 30,000 guilders, who wanted to launch Radio Condor from the vessel and renamed her *Zondaxonagon*, or simply *Condor*. Test transmissions were heard during August 1973, but no regular programmes were ever broadcast. On 31 October 1973, Willemsen sold the vessel to Adriaan Van Landschoot for 50,000 guilders. Then the ship became the home for Radio Atlantis. It was renamed *Jeanine* after Van Landschoot's wife. Radio Atlantis broadcast from 23 December 1973 to 31 August 1974, from international waters off the coast of Belgium.

On 28 April 1976, the *Jeanine* was sold at auction to shipbuilder and demolition company Van de Marel of Ouwerkerk, Holland, and the ship was broken up.

MV *King David* – Capital Radio 1970

The *King David* began life as a 359-ton 148-foot coaster *Unitas*, later called *Zeevaart*, and was built in Groningen, Netherlands, in 1938 by Noord Ned Shipyard. In 1969, the vessel was purchased for 50,000 guilders. In Groningen harbour, the *Zeevaart*'s hull was rebuilt, a new rudder and screw were also installed and, in March 1970, she sailed from Groningen harbour to Zaandam, where the ex-Radio 270 equipment was installed. A new type of loop aerial was installed, suspended from a mast amidship; it was originally designed by the US intelligence and produced only a ground wave.

The ship was then renamed the *King David* and registered in Liechtenstein, the first vessel to fly the country's flag.

Capital Radio only survived as a radio ship for a short time. Test transmissions were carried out from May to August 1970, and regular programmes broadcast from the beginning of September to 9 November 1970, when the ship ran aground and beached at Nordwijk, 200 yards from the Palace Hotel.

On 13 November, the Wijsmuller tug *Hector* towed the MV *King David* clear of the beach. On 18 November, the vessel was taken to Westerdock, Amsterdam. On 26 November, police and harbour authorities served a writ on the ship on behalf of the Wijsmuller company for the salvage fee for towing the MV *King David* off the beach at Noordwijk. The International Broadcasters Society had problems with the insurance company paying out for the salvage fees. The MV *King David* was towed to Betuwe, province of Gelderland, Holland, where it was used as a warehouse for a steel company. In 1972, the ship was auctioned and sold to a ship yard in Heerwaarden, Holland. The *King David* sank in 1994.

MV *Magdalena* – Radio Mi Amigo

Radio Mi Amigo left the MV *Mi Amigo* in October 1978, and a new organisation behind the station set up its own operation from aboard the MV *Magdalena*. The ship, formerly *Centricity*, was built in 1955 at Wallsend for F. T. Everard & Sons of London to carry grain. The 655-ton ship was 191 feet long and 28 feet wide. In 1977, the ship was sold to Internavo Company Ltd. She was registered in Cyprus and renamed *Demi*. One year later, the ship was sold to Magdalena Shipping and Commercial Enterprises of Honduras, who renamed the ship *Magdalena*.

Radio Mi Amigo broadcast on 272 metres medium wave. The station went on-air 1 July 1979, staffed by two Belgian DJs and four Dutchmen, and the programmes were aimed at a Flemish speaking audience. She ceased broadcasting on 18 September 1979. By the following morning, the *Magdalena* had drifted 28 miles into Dutch territitrial waters. She finally ran aground on the Aardappelenbult Sandbank, off Zeeland, Holland. The police launch *Delfshaven* went out and arrested the radio ship.

The *Magdalena* was taken in tow by the tug *Furie II* to the harbour at Stellendam. On 26 September, she was taken to the salvage and demolition company Van der Marel at Oewerkerk, where she was burned and broken up into scrap metal. The same company also scrapped the MV *Caroline* (Radio Caroline North), MV *Comet* (Radio Scotland) and MV *Jeanine* (Radio Atlantis).

MV *MEBO II* – Radio Northsea International

In 1969, Swiss businessmen Edwin Bollier and Erwin Meister bought the 124-foot, 347-ton *Bjarkoy* and renamed her *MEBO*. The ship had been built in Norway. It served as a supply tender to a larger ship they bought later, a Dutch freighter named *Silvretta*, built in 1948 by De Groot and Vliet at Slikkerveer Holland. She was 630 tons and 186 feet long. The ship was purchased for £25,000 and renamed *MEBO II*, and then converted into a radio ship in the same shipyard that built her. A further £65,000 was spent on the conversion.

The Radio Northsea International ship
MEBO II crossing the North Sea for the
Essex coast, 24 March 1970.

MV *MEBO II* left Slikkerveer for an anchorage off the Dutch coast on 22 January 1970. The following night, test transmissions began on 6,210 kHz and 102 mHz. Announcements were made in English for Radio Northsea International by Roger Day, and in German for Radio Noordzee International by Horst Reiner.

The station began regular programmes on 28 February 1970 in both German and English.

On 23 March, *MEBO II* set sail for the English coast, anchoring off Clacton the following morning.

Medium wave broadcasts interfered with the Walton-on-the-Naze coastguards' radio transmissions to Trinity House vessels.

Medium wave transmissions from *MEBO II* were switched off at lunchtime on 27 March. The station returned on 102 mHz and 1,578 kHz, 190 metres medium wave. A more detailed story of RNI can be found in Chapter 2 – The Seventies.

After the Dutch Marine Offences Act came into force on 1 September 1974, it was planned *MEBO II* would enter harbour for an overhaul at the De Groot van Vliet shipyard, then sail to Italy and broadcast as Radio Nova International from the gulf of Genoa. The *MEBO II* arrived at the shipyard on 9 September. Customs officials sealed the cabins, in which the records and other studio equipment had been placed. The *MEBO II* was dry-docked, and 12 inches of crustation was removed from the ship's hull. On 10 October, both *MEBO II* and the *Angela* were seized. The new Dutch laws did not permit ships to carry transmitters except for maritime communications. On 10 December, the courts decided that both ships could leave port once the transmitters had been removed from the *MEBO II*. It was pointed out the *MEBO II* was registered in Panama, and transmitters counted as cargo. On 25 March 1975, the appeal was heard and it was

agreed that the ship was under the jurisdiction of Panamanian law. On 2 January 1976, the court case was finally settled, under the condition that the *MEBO II* sailed within two months and would not transmit from European waters for two years. A bond of 250,000 guilders was ordered and they were fined 5,000 guilders for having a radio ship in Holland after the 31 August 1974. In November 1976, both ships were dry-docked again, the hulls cleaned and repainted.

On 10 January 1977, both ships tested their engines by sailing around the harbour. On 14 January, they left the harbour and sailed down the canal towards Rotterdam. A new crew was taken on while in Rotterdam, and supplies were taken on board at Slikkerveer harbour. On 16 January, the *Angela* headed seaward, followed by the *MEBO II*. Captain van der Kamp was put in charge of both ships. On 20 January, both ships took shelter off Brest, France, for eight days due to bad weather. On 1 February, both ships entered the Mediterranean Sea. On 2 February, they took on supplies in Ceuta, Morocco. On 14 February, both ships entered the harbour, the crew of Cape Verde Islanders were paid off and another Dutch captain took over.

Both ships were bought by Colonel Ghadaffi while land-based transmitters were installed by MEBO Ltd for broadcasting programmes on behalf of the Socialist People's Libyan Arab Jamahiriyah Broadcasting Corporation. In April 1978, the *MEBO II* was renamed *El Fatah*, and was now owned by the Libyan Government. Broadcasts continued until August 1978.

In 1984, both the *Almasira* (ex-*Angela*) and the *El Fatah* (ex-*MEBO II*) were used for target practice by the Libyan Navy. The ships sank in the Gulf of Sidra, Mediterranean Sea.

MV *Mi Amigo* – Radio Caroline South

She is the most famous of the British offshore radio ships. She began life as a three-masted cargo ship. She was built in 1921 by Deutsche Werke in Kiel, Germany, and named SS *Margarethe*.

She sailed around various Baltic Ports carrying general cargo before she was sold and renamed the *Olga* in 1927. Nine years later, she was lengthened to 111 feet 3 inches by adding a new centre section.

During the Second World War, she was requisitioned by the Kriegsmarine, one of three official branches of the Wehrmacht, the armed forces of Nazi Germany. The *Olga* served as an auxiliary ship between 1941 and 1943. She was decommissioned on 18 November 1943. Ten years later, she was again lengthened, this time to 133 feet 9 inches.

Her life as an offshore radio ship came about in 1959, and she was renamed *Bon Jour*. She was fitted out at Norder Werft's shipyard in Hamburg. In June 1960, her cargo hold was converted into studios. The shipyard received a letter, informing them that it was illegal to install, repair or operate a radio station without government approval, a law that had been passed in 1930. The ship then sailed to Denmark, where a radio mast and two 10 kW transmitters were installed.

In February 1961, the *Bon Jour* sailed to Orno, Sweden, and she began broadcasting as Radio Nord. On 2 March 1961, the Swedish government passed a law that enabled them to confiscate all broadcasting equipment on board the ship. She then sailed into international waters off Stockholm.

Radio Nord carried on broadcasting until 30 June 1962, when it was closed by the Swedish authorities. A law had been passed prohibiting Swedes from supplying offshore radio ships with stores, or from providing advertising services to the stations. The ship was put up for sale. The new owners named her *Mi Amigo* and she sailed to Galverston, Texas, where she was to be converted to a luxury yacht. She arrived on 4 March 1962, and her studios were gutted and all broadcasting equipment removed in preparation for conversion to a yacht.

But the yacht never appeared, as Allan Crawford from Project Atlanta wanted to buy the ship for offshore broadcasting in the United Kingdom. It was December 1963 before Crawford could raise the necessary capital. The *Mi Amigo* then sailed to Spain, where she arrived at the end of January 1964. Her next port of call was Greenore, Ireland, where a 141-foot mast was erected. She then sailed to the Essex coast, arriving on 27 April 1964 off Frinton-on-Sea, and began broadcasting as Radio Atlanta. Radio Caroline had already begun broadcasting on 28 March from international waters off Felixstowe, Suffolk.

On 2 July 1964, Radio Atlanta merged with Radio Caroline and the *Mi Amigo* became the home of Radio Caroline South. The *Fredericia*, renamed, MV *Caroline*, sailed to an anchorage off the Isle of Man and became Radio Caroline North.

The *Mi Amigo* hit the news headlines on 20 January 1966 when she drifted in a Force 8 gale, ending up in a snowstorm on the beach at Holland-on-Sea. The DJs and crew on board were rescued by Breeches buoy. The *Mi Amigo* was refloated and sailed to Zaandam, Netherlands, for repairs. She returned to her anchorage off the Essex coast and recommenced broadcasting on 16 April 1964.

The Marine Offences Act became law at midnight on 14 August 1967. On 3 March 1968, the tug *Titan* drew alongside the *Mi Amigo,* and Radio Caroline South was ordered to close down. At a similar time, Radio Caroline North was ordered to close down. Both ships were seized by the Offshore Company as security for the £30,000 that they owed, and towed to Amsterdam.

On 29 May 1972, the *Mi Amigo* was sold at auction for £20,000 to the Hofman Shipping Company. She set sail on 2 September 1972 and arrived off Scheveningen. Broadcasts did take place, but no regular programming was heard. Station identifications included Radio 199 and Radio Caroline and, later still, Radio Mi Amigo and Radio Seagull.

To coincide with the introduction of the Dutch Marine Offences Act, coming in to force at the end of August, the *Mi Amigo* sailed across the North Sea, accompanied by the *Delta Diving,* owned by Captain Tom van der Linden, to the Thames Estuary. On 14 November 1975, the ship was boarded by British police and Home Office officials, who ordered that broadcasting should stop. The studio microphone was switched on and, at 2.50 p.m., listeners heard a scuffle. At one minute past three, the station abruptly left the air. The captain, two DJs and an engineer were taken off the ship by Detective Sergeant Hargreaves to Southend police station, where they were charged with offences under the Marine Offences Act.

The *Mi Amigo* remained at sea, but on 19 March 1980, her anchor chain broke in a Force 10 storm and she drifted some

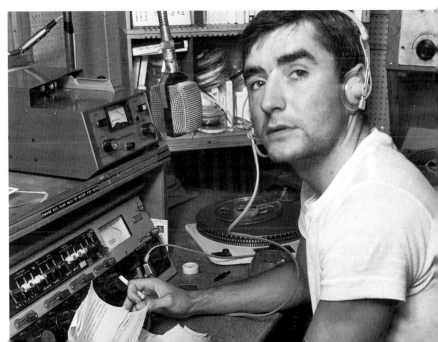

Above right: The *Mi Amigo* off the Essex coast in the mid-1970s.

Below right: Steve Young regularly filled the midnight to six slot on Radio Caroline between 1966 and 1967.

10 nautical miles, ending up aground on the Long Sandbank. The ship sank on 20 March, leaving only her radio mast above the water. This mast collapsed at the end of July 1986. The *Mi Amigo*, now a wreck, lies at the bottom of the North Sea, but is marked by a buoy. A sad ending to a ship that had such a varied and interesting life.

MV *Oceaan 7* – Radio 270

The *Oceaan 7* was built in 1939 by A. Vuijk and Zonen Sons of Capelle in the Netherlands, a company founded in 1872, and was 139 feet long and weighed 160 tons. The ship was used by the Dutch fishing fleet of Scheveningen as *Scheveningen 333*. During the Second World War, the Germans captured the ship and used her as a transportation vessel. After the war, the ship was handed back to the Dutch fishing fleet, where she was used until 1964. It was a sister ship of Radio Delmare's *Aegir II*.

In 1965, the vessel was purchased in Holland. The total cost price for the entire project was £75,000 pounds. This was incredibly low for a complete offshore radio station. The *Oceaan 7* was registered in Puerto Rico (Honduras).

The ship then sailed to international waters, 3 miles off the Scarborough coast, arriving on 26 February 1966. Storms in the North Sea prevented Radio 270 from beginning to broadcast. The *Oceaan 7* then moved location to 3 miles off Bridlington. The station went on-air 4 June 1966 and closed down on 14 August 1967

After the Marine Offences Act came into operation, the *Oceaan 7* sailed to Whitby harbour under the command of Ken Lester. The broadcasting equipment and transmitting mast were removed from the ship. The ship was put up for sale by Tuckley & Co. of Whitby and Scarborough for the sum of £25,000. In March 1968, the ship nearly became a temporary home for Radio Caroline, but the national press had leaked the story, and the owners of the *Oceaan 7* were threatened with prosecutions if broadcasts resumed. Eventually, the ship was sold as scrap for £5,000, and was broken up at Blyth, Northumberland.

MV *Olga Patricia* renamed *Laissez-Faire* – Britain Radio and Radio England

The *Olga Patricia* was built in New York in 1944, as a 480-ton landing craft 186 feet long. During the Korean War, the cargo vessel was used to carry the bodies of GIs killed in Korea back to the USA.

In early 1966, the *Olga Patricia* was purchased by William Vick of London. The ship sailed from the Panama Canal zone to Dodge Island shipyard at Biscayne Bay, Miami, where she was fitted out as a radio ship. The station would transmit programmes from two stations – Radio England and Britain Radio. The *Olga Patricia* sailed to British waters and anchored near Radio Caroline South and Radio London. Test transmissions on both stations began on 3 May 1966. Regular programmes for both Radio England and Britain Radio began on 18 June 1966. Programmes were transmitted through two separate aerials, held aloft by a 210-foot mast.

Although both stations were initially very popular with listeners, they lacked revenue. Radio England closed on

MV *Olga Patricia* renamed
Laissez-Faire off the coast of
Frinton-on-Sea, Essex, in 1967.

13 November 1966 and was replaced by Radio Dolfijn, which transmitted programmes in Dutch from November 1966 to March 1967, when she changed her call sign to Radio 227. This station closed on 23 July 1967. Britain Radio closed on 22 February 1967 and was replaced by Radio 355, which ceased broadcasting on 5 August 1967.

The *Olga Patricia* was renamed *Laissez-Faire* in March 1967.

MV *Peace* formerly MV *Cito* – Voice of Peace

Beginning life as the MV *Rolf*, built in early 1940, she was the very last ship to leave Delfzijl harbour in the north-east of the Netherlands before the German invasion in May 1940. The ship was built at the Van Diepen shipyard in Waterhuizen, Netherlands, weighing 400 tons. The length of the ship was 177 feet, with a width of 28 feet and a depth of 8 feet. In those days, the vessel could carry 38 tons of fuel and travel at 11 knots an hour.

In 1950, the ship was renamed MV *Westpolder*. In 1954, the ship was taken to the same wharf where she was built. Here, some adjustments were made on the bridge. The ship mainly made trips in European waters, and to Madeira and countries around the Mediterranean. It was in 1960 that the ship got her new name – MV *Cito*. The former Dutch cargo ship was converted to an offshore radio station and, on 12 August 1969, was renamed MV *Peace*. The output was popular music, presented by mostly British and Australian DJs, who broadcast live from the ship.

Dutch media authority Hans Knot remembers the vessel was his local playground in Groningen. He recalls:

In my teens, with some of my friends, I listened to offshore radio stations like Radio London, Radio Caroline, Swinging Radio England and more. We were not the only ones. In the city of Groningen, my hometown, some avid radio listeners were already publicly showing their interest. In 1966, for instance, on the wall of a shed at the Gorechtkade, someone painted in capital letters: 'Radio London on 266.' In June 2014, like I normally do once a year, I again checked if the shed was still there. It was. The surroundings carry more memories to offshore radio. Some 350 metres away from that shed is a canal called the 'Oosterhamrikkanaal'.

In the late sixties there were two ships at the quayside, moored next to each other – the MV *Zeevaart* and the MV *Cito*. Both ships were waiting for a new future and new owners and were for sale. We could be found a lot playing around those ships, as it was only 350 metres away from our home. The first ship, believe it or not, would become the radio ship for Capital Radio of the International Broadcasters Society, and would be renamed into MV *King David*. The latter one was the MV *Cito*, which in 1969 would be renamed the MV *Peace*.

It was very exciting to see these vessels turned into offshore radio stations much later in my life.

The Voice of Peace was founded by Abraham 'Abie' Nathan, an Israeli humanitarian and peace activist. He bought the *Cito*, and on 12 August 1969 the former Dutch cargo ship was renamed MV *Peace*. It belonged to shipowners Paap from Haren, a village near Groningen. Partners in the company were H. Paap and W. J. van Wijk, and with the latter Abie Nathan had signed the contract for the sale to the Peace Foundation. The price for the ship was £16,500.

She later sailed from Holland to the United States to be converted into a floating radio station. She anchored in New York harbour and a 50kW transmitter was installed with a 160-foot aerial. The ship departed New York on 16 March 1973. Test transmissions were carried out in the Atlantic on 195 metres, 1,549 kHz. She arrived in Marseilles in mid-April, and later sailed around various locations in the Middle East.

It anchored off Tel Aviv and broadcast from 19 May 1973 to 1 October 1993, with a break from November 1973 to June 1975 due to a shortage of money.

The main on-air studio comprised a Gates Diplomat mixer, Technics SL-1200 turntables, Sony CD players and Gates NAB cartridge machines, on which the jingles and commercials were played. The second studio, for production, had a Gates turntable, reel-to-reel tape recorders and an NAB cartridge recording unit.

The final days of the VOP took place when Abie Nathan decided that because the Israeli Government and the PLO were talking to each other, there was no need for the VOP anymore. However, there was also another reason. The station's debts were mounting, there was competition from Israeli legal stations and the soon-to-be introduced local commercial stations in Israel, all of which played a part in the closure of the Voice of Peace.

On 1 October 1993, the Voice of Peace began her last day of broadcasting. The mayor of Tel Aviv went out to the ship and broadcast live, promising an anchorage for the MV *Peace* in Tel Aviv harbour, and the ship would be rebuilt as a peace museum. The station closed with 'We Shall Overcome' by Pete Seeger. The station transmitters were switched off at 2.57 p.m.

For the next few days, the MV *Peace* remained anchored off the coast of Tel Aviv, waiting to be taken into port and converted into a museum. However, the government kept changing its mind over plans for the ship. While still offshore, the transmitters were run and several test broadcasts were made. However, Abie Nathan grew impatient and ordered the studios and transmitters to be dismantled.

Afterwards, the MV *Peace* sailed to Ashdod, 32 kilometres south of Tel Aviv in the Mediterranean, where equipment was removed from the ship. Abie Nathan was convinced that there would be no peace in the Middle East for the forseeable future, so he decided to scuttle the ship. On 28 November 1993, the MV *Peace* set sail on her final voyage, 15 miles off the Israeli coast. The hull plugs were removed from the engine room and lower hold, and the pumps switched on, to force water into the ship.

At 7.33 p.m., the MV *Peace* sank. Abie Nathan died in Tel Aviv on 27 August 2008, at the age of eighty-one.

The station was later relaunched as an online land-based station in August 2009, and in 2014 a second online channel was added, called the Voice of Peace Classics.

MV *Ross Revenge* – Radio Caroline

The *Ross Revenge*, formally the MV *Freyr*, was built in 1960 by A. G. Weser Werk, Seebeck, Bremerhaven, West Germany, as a trawler. The ship was 223 feet in length, 34 feet wide and weighed 963 tons.

Until August 1963, the ship was owned by the Icelandic company Isbjorninn. Then the *Freyr* was sold to the Ross Trawlers Ltd/Ross

Fisheries and renamed *Revenge* GY 718 (home harbour Grimsby). It was the world's largest conventional trawler and involved in the Icelandic cod war of 1 September 1972 to 1 June 1976. On return to Grimsby, the Ross Group renamed her *Ross Revenge*. Due to extended limits, dwindling catches, quotas and foreign imports, it was becoming uneconomic to use such a large trawler. From 1979 to 1981, the vessel served as diving support ship in the North Sea.

In 1981, the MV *Ross Revenge* was moored at the Cairnryan breakers yard in Rosyth, Scotland, and was found to be suitable for the Radio Caroline project. The company Seamore from Liechtenstein purchased the MV *Ross Revenge* from Silas Victor Oates (based in Guernsey) for only £28,500. The ship was then registered in Panama.

In April 1981, the *Ross Revenge* was towed by the Spanish tug *Aznar Jose Luis* from the Cairnryan breakers yard and arrived in Solares, near Santander (Spain), five days later. In autumn 1981, work began on converting the *Ross Revenge* into a radio ship. The transmitter mast was the tallest mast ever to be fitted to a ship, 300 feet above sea level. The main transmitter was a RCA Ampliphase Model BTA 50H (serial number 101).

On 4 August 1983, the *Ross Revenge*, under the command of Captain Martin Eve, headed for the Thames Estuary and anchored in the Kentish Knock on 8 August. The following day, the ship moved anchorage to the Knock John Deep. The *Ross Revenge* had a colourful career as a radio ship. More details about its broadcasts can be found in Chapter 3 – The Eighties.

The *Ross Revenge* was used as a radio ship for Caroline from 20 August 1983 to 5 November 1990. Other stations that broadcast from the ship were Radio Monique (1984–87), World Mission Radio (1988/89), Radio 558 (1988) and Radio 819 (1988/89).

The ship was also used for Radio Caroline Restricted Service Licence broadcasts, including Dover, Chatham, Burnham-on-Crouch, Bradwell, Clacton-on-Sea, Canary Wharf, London, Rochester, Queenborough and Southend-on-Sea.

The *Ross Revenge* was anchored in the River Blackwater, off Essex, in October 1993. She moved to a new location in Queenborough, on the Isle of Sheppey in August 1997. On 30 July 2004, the ship was towed to the Port of Tilbury in Essex, where she was berthed for ten years. On 31 July 2014, she was moved to a new location near Bradwell, Essex, in the River Blackwater.

Chapter 6
THE LEGEND STILL LIVES ON

By Sir Hans Knot

Sir Hans Knot (1949) is a media historian from the Netherlands, researching and writing since 1969. From the early days of Offshore Radio, he followed all that was happening on the stations, collecting everything and making friends with those working on the stations. He has written forty-five books on media history and music culture, and contributed to many more. He was also one of the three people responsible for organising the yearly RadioDays from 1978 up until 2014. He also worked for almost four decades at the University of Groningen, until September 2014, and still has some honorary tasks there today. On 29 April 2009, he was knighted by the then Dutch Queen Beatrix in Order of the House of Orange for his outstanding work in highlighting part of Dutch media culture history.

When the Marine Offences Act became law in August 1967 in the UK, as well as the so-called 'Anti Zeezenderwet' brought in by the Dutch government in September 1974, everybody thought that public radio had won, and the millions of listeners to offshore radio would find their way either to the BBC or the stations in Hilversum. Commercial radio was planned in the UK, but it took until 1973 before a few of the independent radio stations made a start. In the Netherlands, it even took more time before the first official commercial radio station started at the end of 1988.

But everyone who thought that the closing down of the offshore radio stations meant free radio was done with was wrong. Radio Caroline went on in the sixties until a temporary end came when both ships – the MV *Mi Amigo* and MV *Fredericia* – were towed from their anchorage in international waters to Amsterdam harbour, due to large debts to their tendering company.

After 31 August 1974, when stations like Veronica, RNI and Radio Atlantis went off the air, the reborn Radio Caroline went on, together with its sister station Radio Mi Amigo. This was possible due to the owner, Belgian Sylvain Tack, making payments for tendering and salaries until October 1978. Radio Caroline then came into trouble again, went off the air, and had to search for new backers. At Easter 1979, the station was on the air again, this time with Dutch backers and religious organisations from the USA, who provided the money to survive.

They were not the only ones, as a part of the Mi Amigo organisation bought a new ship, the MV *Magdalena*, and started programmes in 1979 off the Belgian coast. The wrong anchorage, together with an ill-chosen crew, led to a very sudden closure after just a few weeks. An undersized anchor chain caused the ship to drift into Dutch waters, and she was arrested. It meant the end of Mi Amigo 272. Others, headed by Dutchmen Gerard van Dam, who was already active for RNI in 1970 and Caroline in 1972 as well as Atlantis in 1973, started Radio Delmare. In its 100 days on the air, broadcasting from several ships, the Radio Delmare was the most ill-fated pirate radio station off the Dutch coast.

The stations had a lot of followers, and in four different countries there were special magazines in which offshore radio was highlighted. To mention a few of them, we start with *Monitor Magazine*, first published in 1972 and headed by Roland C. 'Buster' Pearson. He was assisted by Penelope Page (Jeanne Scyra). 'Buster' not only listened to radio, but was also a trusted contact between the organisations on land and the DJs and crew members on the radio ships. *Monitor Magazine*, which followed everything happening on the offshore radio stations in the 1970s and 1980s, was mentioned a lot on-air. It also gained a huge interest from other countries, and so the readership grew with each issue. Buster had haemophilia, and so radio was a friendly companion for him. Sadly, he died on 23 December 1985, aged fifty-seven. Jeanne, and her friend Don Scott, decided to go on with *Monitor Magazine*, and others also stepped in to ensure its success, including offshore photographer Theo Dencker, Dutch reporter Arie van der Kust (Karel Gerbers) and Hans Knot, who wrote about the Dutch offshore stations in the past and present. After a name change to *Newscaster*, the last issue appeared in 1991. An exclusive interview with Buster by Chris Edwards, from *Offshore Echos* magazine, can be found at http://www.offshoreechos.com/Buster-Jean.htm.

In *Offshore Echos*, we have another magazine related to pirate radio. It was first published in 1974, as a duplicated newsletter written in French by the France Radio Club. As the readership grew, the magazine expanded. English, Dutch and German language sections were added and, by the end of 1982, the English language section had grown to such an extent that it was necessary to produce two separate magazines. Two important names have to be mentioned, François Lhote and Chris Edwards, who are the main editors. In 2013, the French edition closed. Other people followed to help them to bring in news, information and interviews, among them Robert Magniez, Baudouin Dom and Hans Knot. The latter two are still writing for *Offshore Echos* in 2014.

In February 1995, *Offshore Echos* celebrated with a special colour magazine to mark its 100th edition, and FRC's twenty-first anniversary.

Offshore Echos is unique in being the only magazine in the world solely devoted to offshore radio. Its readers are international, spanning more than twenty-five countries and comprising not only listeners but also radio industry professionals.

France Radio Club is looking at all means – financial, logistical and material – to allow an offshore station to come back on the air from the North Sea, and keep alive the spirit of free radio and adventure at sea – the concept of offshore radio for today's and future generations.

For many years, France Radio Club hosted the Euroradio convention – a meeting of free radio enthusiasts from across Europe, allowing them to join personalities from the offshore radio scene past and present. Euroradio was first held in Calais in July 1990, and was held annually until September 2011. One of the main aims of France Radio Club is to collect as much archive material (sound, film, video, paperwork, documents, photographs, etc.) on the subject of offshore radio and its history, and make these available to the public. It has helped numerous media sources, including television and radio, with research on the offshore stations. France Radio Club has also regularly participated in various debates on radio.

A short mention also has to be given to a publication that came out in the 1980s, called *Anoraks UK*. This free radio organisation, based in Blackpool, used to publish a weekly report of pirate radio stations in the UK and Eire, including Radio Caroline and Laser 558. *Anoraks UK* also sold airchecks and other free radio memorabilia.

Radio Review is another magazine partly devoted to the love of offshore radio. Founder Geoff Baldwin wrote in the International Radio Report early in 2014:

Just one of the reasons for following this station so closely in the 1970s and 1980s was its anti-establishment credentials, both in broadcasting and broader terms and not wanting to be told what radio station I had to listen to! That brings me to the other information that came to light when I was researching about the early 1960s history of Radio Caroline. The focus always tends to be on the DJs and those who were most in the public eye, but those that may have been involved in some way 'behind the scenes' have always had less attention and are unknown to most offshore radio enthusiasts.

An example of this is the actual people who put up the original £250,000 (the equivalent of £4.6 million in today's money) to get Radio Caroline on the air (and who, effectively, owned Planet Productions) – they are little known by anoraks. They were very much part of not just the business world, but the British establishment. One of the main backers was an aristocrat whose family even had Royal connections and was a close relative of the current British Prime Minister's wife Samantha Cameron! The other main backer had run the family fisheries company that went on to own a fleet of trawlers, including the *Ross Revenge*! More recently, this second backer's grandson has also been in the public eye because he helped set up a well-known mobile phone retailer some years ago, which has helped him become a multi-millionaire and one of the richest people in Britain – he has also been involved with our current Prime Minister David Cameron (when the latter was still leader of the opposition) as a fundraiser for the Conservative party.

So, not only would Radio Caroline not have got on the air in 1964 without these establishment figures providing the initial capital to fund the project, but this was the start of the family/

friend links to the heart of the UK establishment that have continued into modern times – indeed, to the current occupants of No. 10 Downing Street, the Prime Minister and his wife!

This is just one of the many opinions Geoff Baldwin wrote through the past decades for *Radio Review*, which has published more than 230 issues.

Howard C. Rose, better known as DJ Crispian St John and Jay Jackson, was a larger-than-life character, and was obsessed with radio from an early age. He worked as an offshore DJ on RNI (1971), Radio Caroline (1972), Radio Atlantis (1973) and Voice of Peace (1976–81). When Independent Local Radio was established in the UK, he worked for a number of stations.

Apart from broadcasting, he founded and edited the *Radio Magazine* from 1991, until it was sold in 2002. A great broadcaster, a positive radio anorak and a personal friend, he sadly died of a heart attack in 2002, at the age of forty-nine.

In the Netherlands in 1968, *Pirate Radio News* was founded – an organisation headed by Willem Herrebrugh, a later member of the Dutch Parliament, Dick van Schenk Brill and Jacob Kokje. The aim was to bring news and rumours from the world of free radio to listeners of the offshore and pirate radio stations. They published, at first irregularly, an info bulletin, which later became more regular. After sending in some newsflashes, the writer of this article was asked to join the editorial staff, and soon became the final editor of

Right: The *Ross Revenge*.

the *Pirate Radio News*. This led to many contacts in the field of radio, and visits were made to the studios on land as well as visits to some of the radio ships. The magazine continued until the summer of 1976, when I was already writing for a Belgian publication, *Baffle*. This radio and offshore radio bulletin soon became *RadioVisie*, for which the main men were Jean Luc Bostyn from Belgium and Frans Schuurbiers from the Netherlands. Other writers were Bert Bossink and Jelle Boonstra. From a printed magazine, it changed into a daily internet news magazine from 2000. After four decades, *RadioVisie* ceased publication in June 2013.

In 1978, Freddy Jorus from Merksem in Belgium, Ton van Draanen from Amsterdam and Hans Knot from Groningen decided to take over the ill-fated magazine *Freeway* and rebuild it into the *Freewave Media Magazine*. Firstly, it was a three-weekly magazine, later a monthly, with news from public, commercial, as well as offshore radio. Several people within the radio industry were invited to cooperate with the editorial staff, and one of the main topics was to write articles with a historical background. In April 2014, the name of the magazine was changed into *Freewave Nostalgia*. I'm still the final editor of this magazine.

But there were more interesting ways to communicate with the offshore fans – or anoraks – such as telephone lines where you could dial a number to get the weekly information. Of course, you had to pay for it, and part of the money went to the organiser of such a phone service. Two to mention were the phone service from Radio Caroline manager Peter Moore, and the one from John Burch, running the Jaybee Enterprises from Grays in Essex.

It was in June 1994, as a result of the popularity of the offshore radio stations, that a special exhibition was opened in the Hilversum Broadcasting Museum. For those who didn't know, the last offshore broadcast in Europe was made – at that stage – in 1990. During almost six months, thousands of people from all over the Netherlands and Belgium, as well as from Germany and Great Britain, took the time to swim in a nostalgia of artefacts, photos, audio sounds, videos, posters, T-shirts and much more. The exhibition got enormous attention in the press in the Netherlands as well as on radio and television. The main men behind the organisation were Arno Weltens and Hans Knot.

The exhibition was officially opened with the presentation of a double CD by ex-Veronica programme director Joost den Draayer (Willem van Kooten), and one of the three former Veronica directors, Hendrik 'Bull' Verweij. The double CD 'Het grote Bull Verweij verhaal' was a compilation of a session of seventeen hours of interviews done by Jelle Boonstra and Hans Knot with 'Bull' Verweij. He told his life story, and it was edited on two CDs by Jelle Boonstra.

During the past two decades, several programmes were broadcast by the so-called RSL (Restricted Short Licensed) stations. Offshore stations from the past were remembered several times by former DJs from the stations, and by volunteers who made their first steps into radio. Some of these special RSLs were from ships anchored in international waters, others from a ship in a harbour or on a quayside. One example was RNI, which returned as an RSL station in August 1999. From the third of that month up until the thirtieth, the station broadcast from the *LV18*, a former Trinity House lightship. During this

RSL, the *LV18* was nicknamed *MEBO III*. It was towed to a position off the Holland-on-Sea coast, and the station was on the air on 190 metres medium wave, 1,575 kHz. During the RSL, the DJs remembered the music from the 1970s.

Some former offshore DJs and technicians participated in the venture: Paul Graham, Paul MacLaren, Alan West, Norman Barrington, Dick Palmer, Dennis Jason, Bob Noakes, Kevin Turner, Bob LeRoi, Ray Anderson, Dave Rodgers, Dave West and Phil Mitchell. Together with Graham Vine, Chris Baird, Clive Boutell, Mike Read and Colin Lamb, they made the RSL a big success. In 2001, Tony Currie wrote an excellent story, 'Living in the Past', about this and other RSLs for the online *Journal for Media and Music Culture* at the University Groningen.

Several organisations came on the market with offshore radio related products. I like to mention three of them. Earlier a mention was made for *Offshore Echos* magazine. Its editorial staff also produced several CDs as well as videos, later revised versions on DVD, all about the history of offshore radio. Another organisation in London, which first produced LPs with offshore radio extracts under the name 'Jumbo Records and Tapes', later changed location to Frinton-on-Sea and still is in operation today.

It was in 1978 that Rob Olthof, together with two other persons, founded *Media Communications* in Amsterdam. During the period 1971 until 1978, he already had organised – in cooperation with the team from *Pirate Radio News* – several boat trips to the offshore radio stations, and released several records. The Foundation for Media Communications also released a lot of videos, CDs and documentaries, and was responsible for the many trips to the radio ships off the British coast in the 1980s. He organised these trips together with Leen Vingerling. But the Foundation for Media Communication is best known for two other activities. It has published more than fifty books about the history of offshore radio, partly in Dutch and partly in English. It also organised the RadioDays from 1978 until 2014. The organisers were Hans Knot, Martin van der Ven and the late Rob Olthof. Its most successful event was held in Amsterdam in March 2014, when over 500 media personalities and radio enthusiasts from around the world attended.

Next to a lot of devoted internet sites about offshore radio, in the late 1990s I got the idea to start an international monthly newsletter to answer a lot of questions and give the reader a platform to bring in their own memories. The *Hans Knot International Radio Report* was born and brought a lot of people, who had totally lost each other for more than thirty-five years, back together. A lot of untold stories were published, as well an ocean of unique photographic material. More than 4,000 readers around the world get the report by email, and it can be found on a couple of internet sites.

Barbara Apostolides, a keen radio listener from the beginning of English offshore stations:

199 Caroline … 199 Caroline…

Oh drat, I muttered, for I was searching for Radio Veronica on 192, a tuneful radio station that I had discovered while searching the wavelength of my teeny radio for something tuneful as opposed to the somewhat droll and dry BBC Light, Home and Third programmes, none of which suited my need for bright, cheerful music during the daytime.

Drat, drat and drat. For a few days, all I could pick up was 199 Caroline, not a station but the threat of a new one, which obliterated my beloved Veronica. Drat!

Then out of the blue came music, singers, instrumentals and radio presenters who stopped short of just announcing a record but would give out details of the singer, often adding off the cuff remarks, silly remarks that would often tally with happenings in one's home – as a listener, one felt a sense of belonging. I think most of the amusing happenings connected with the offshore stations have been well documented, although there were minor events that made one chuckle. Such as the occasion I plugged the toaster into the same point as the radio – the voice of Keith Skues instantly filled the kitchen saying, 'Gosh it's getting hot in here.'

The DJs encouraged us to join in, send comments, write letters. We became one big family. I was hooked and rarely missed a programme, except that is, on the day of a severe storm that wiped out Caroline's signal; all I could hear was Radio Veronica on 192 … oh drat!

Tony Blackburn, DJ Radio Caroline South, Radio London, BBC Radios 1 and 2, local BBC and commercial stations:

I loved Radio Caroline and thought the station was great. If it hadn't been for Caroline, I don't think I would have ended up in radio. When I first saw the Caroline South ship *Mi Amigo* in 1964, I became quite excited realising that we could change the whole of broadcasting and break the BBC monopoly. On board, we were able to sit down for hours and learn all about spinning records and playing commercials and presenting a three-hour radio show, without scripts. I owe everything I now have to Radio Caroline, where I worked for two years, and then one year on Radio London. They were great days.

We were the youngest people in broadcasting in this country at that time in the 1960s. I was twenty-one when I started broadcasting and we were broadcasting to listeners who were our age. We brought a totally different sound to radio, and for the very first time during the day you had non-stop pop music. It was a fantastic time to have been part of the sixties music explosion.

The audience that tuned in to Caroline was massive, and it was the first time a radio station had communicated with its audience, especially teenagers and young housewives.

I believe Radio Caroline was the first reality show, because listeners could tune in to find out what we were doing on the ship, as we all lived together. That is something we cannot create today. We would talk about coping with Force 10 gales, and welcoming any pop star visitors who travelled out on the tender, the meals we were having on board, or that we were going on shore leave for a week.

Two records I remember from the early days of Caroline that became hits through the station were The Honeycombs 'Have I The Right' and Tom Jones 'It's Not Unusual'.

When I talk to teenagers today about radio, the majority had never heard of the pirate radio ships, which is a great pity because that sound will never come back again. Looking back fifty years, the whole experience was very special and I feel proud to have been a part of it.

David Clayton, Editor, BBC Radio Norfolk:

It's the summer of '67, I'm a teenager earning some extra pocket money doing a seasonal job selling ice cream and seaside rock on Gorleston sea front. With my first week's wages I've acquired a transistor radio and it's perched on top of the ice cream fridge with non-stop Radio London coming out of the speaker. I'm dealing with a steady stream of sunburnt customers and staring out at endless sunny days.

I simply loved Radio London. The DJs (including the co-author of this book) were having fun and talking to me not at me. They were my radio pals. I felt I was included in their fun, despite the fact I couldn't text, phone or email them back in those days. Then there was the music. Those wonderful, heady 'summer of love' tunes live long in my memory. For me, they've never been bettered, and what's more, the DJs' enthusiasm for the records they were playing made me love the music even more.

Back then I had no concept of a career in broadcasting. I'm sure I envied the supposed glamorous lifestyles of the DJs. I didn't ever conceive it was a possible career when I was a pupil at Great Yarmouth Grammar School back in the sixties. No careers talk ever mentioned broadcasting.

Fast forward to the seventies and I'm a mobile disco DJ and involved with hospital radio. I realise I'm nearly doing what those

Tony Blackburn in the studio of
Radio Caroline South in 1965.

guys did out on the North Sea. I've got the bug and especially with my early forays on to Hospital Radio Norwich, my radio presenting reference points were all about how the pirates had sounded.

There was no local radio round here until 1980, when BBC Radio Norfolk came along, but I was waiting for it, eager to be involved. Eventually I was. Again, the closer I got to the atmosphere I'd remembered hearing on the pirate stations, the happier I was, and I'm happy to report so were the audience. It wasn't so much about what we were putting out on the airwaves; it was about the relationship with the listeners.

It is well documented that the pirates put a well-placed boot up the backside of traditional broadcasting styles, which was all BBC back in the sixties, and I firmly believe their legacy is still pervading the airwaves today. The foundations of the way we present the music/speech mix of radio was formulated, I believe, by those watery wireless pioneers. Yes it may have developed, morphed and become more sophisticated as technology has moved on, but the roots are still there.

Being privileged to be responsible for a BBC Local Radio station's output, I've been very happy to nod back in the direction of our pirate ancestors whenever an anniversary has presented itself. Famous old pirates have graced BBC Radio Norfolk's airwaves, and our Norfolk audience, who after all faced the sea most of them were broadcasting from, continue to love the nostalgia. That was proved, if ever we doubted it, when on Easter Monday 2014 we brought back Tom Edwards, Ray Clark, Andy Archer, Keith Skues and Colin Berry together in our studios to recreate a whole day of pirate-style broadcasting fifty years on from when Radio Caroline started a new era of broadcasting.

The hair was a bit greyer, if there was any, the studios didn't bob up and down, but the tunes and the voices were firmly from those few golden years of the sixties.

After fifty years, I'm not too sure how many more pirate anniversaries we can celebrate, but don't worry – given the slightest excuse…

Tom Edwards, DJ Radio City, Radio Caroline, BBC Radios 1 and 2, Radio Norfolk:

I first heard Radio Caroline when it began transmission way back at the Easter of 1964. To hear non-stop music and DJs simply ad-libbing was a radio revolution to me and the millions of people tuning in. What made it even more exciting to me was that it was broadcasting from a ship off the East Anglian coast, and as I have always loved music, I wanted to be there. More stations followed, either on ships or the old wartime forts.

I started in 1965 on the Shivering Sands forts, which was broadcasting the programmes of Radio City on 299 metres. These towers still stand and I have long had the ambition to go back and look at them close up after some forty-seven years. I feel they will outlive me, as they have been standing strong for over seventy years. However, a warning from the Ministry of Defence advised me some time ago never to approach them, worse still go on board these awesome looking structures. City was never as big a station as say Radio London, Radio 390 and Radio Caroline (both South and North), but judging by the mail we got we must have been doing something right. On-air we talked to our listeners as friends, which in turn made their many letters and cards to us so satisfying.

I stayed on at City as programme director for two years, and I finally closed down this station for last time in 1967, due to being fined at court. To me it was a heart-breaking moment because I loved Radio City so much, but nothing is forever.

Within weeks, I was on board the *Mi Amigo* ship (Radio Caroline South) meeting all my DJ heroes and enjoying every single moment. However, there was a dark cloud looming in the shape of the Marine Offences Act, which would come into law on 14 August 1967. I left the ship a mere twelve hours before that act became law. I was invited to go back to sea but I never did.

What I got from those three years out at sea in all weathers was the most exciting part of my life. I don't think we actually knew what we were doing at the time apart from standing up to the government, giving millions of listeners a chance to hear the music they wanted and that radio would never ever be the same again.

Even the BBC had to change their wireless output, and thus, in 1967, was born Radios 1, 2, 3 and 4 and, just a few years later, commercial radio on terra firma was allowed to happen. All of this due to those stations broadcasting from the high seas.

Offshore radio continued in various forms and shapes, but those three years from 1964 to 1967 should never ever be forgotten. Nor will the deep friendships we DJs developed all those years ago and are still as strong as they ever were.

I am most proud to have played a small role in something that was a radio revolution, which gave the listening public something they had never heard before and loved every bit of those musical moments as much we did, spinning the vinyl on the turntable(s).

Because there were no computers back then, the pirate radio era is today well remembered with footage of that bygone age now freely available on YouTube or other offshore radio sites.

The memories of those heady times out at sea in all weathers and conditions are there for everyone to see or listen into. That heartens me, because they will now be there forever, which is the way it should be.

Alex Hendricks, airline captain, Brussels, Belgium, and keen radio listener:

Isn't it great that still there is so much interest for those 'pirate years' today. Fifty years ago, you [Keith Skues] and the other DJs really did something that was unheard of then and still captures the minds of people today. I know that even youngsters who were not even born then, hear and read with great interest what was done then – the fight for free radio and the fight to bring 'all-day music' to the airwaves, fought by a group of young enthusiastic DJs, often living in dreadful circumstances on tiny ships floating anchored on the often wild North Sea.

I was, and still am, very happy that I actually was one of the people then who did little more than listen to the offshore stations. In 1964, I was just thirteen years old and bought my first little Sharp transistor radio and became glued to it. Radio Veronica was not my favourite station; it was the British stations, mainly Radio Caroline and 'Big L' Radio London, as their programmes could be received very clearly in Amsterdam, where I lived at the time. Then, when the stations were banned by the British government, it became even more interesting for me … Caroline and its DJs moved to an office at the Singel in Amsterdam! I spoke to them all, frequently hanging out in their office. Spoke to Johnnie Walker and to Robbie Dale frequently (if you Google 'Robbie Dale, Johnnie Walker, Lex Hendriks' you will find a picture of one such meeting). By the way, that picture sitting on a canal bridge fence just outside the Caroline office, was made during an interview I did with them for our school magazine. That interview was (how lucky I was) filmed by a Granada television crew and featured in one of their 'World in Action' programmes on pirate radio.

I also went on a tender from Scheveningen to the good ship *Mi Amigo* still at anchor off the Essex coast. A rough trip, but well worth it. From that moment on, I kept very frequent contact with notably Robbie Dale and Roger Day.

Finally, I boarded many trips to the *MEBO II* when it was off Scheveningen. Nice, big ship and clearly more comfortable than the *Mi Amigo*.

So, pirate radio completely dominated my teenage life. School homework was done with the radio tuned to Caroline or Big L.

Derek James, journalist and feature writer:

There I was, under the bedclothes, fiddling about with my radio. One moment I was listening to Jerry Lee Lewis and then the signal went, to be replaced leaving a sort of hiss. That's the way it was with Radio Luxembourg. One moment great music – the kind most grown-ups hated – the next nothing.

Then, at Easter time, half a century ago, all that changed with the arrival of Radio Caroline, and suddenly the 1960s really did start to swing.

Only those of a certain age will remember the impact it had on so many young lives. It was bold and boisterous. It was like a blast of fresh air. It was if we had our own friends just talking to us on the radio. Broadcasting had changed forever.

At last those stuffed shirts at the BBC realised there was a young generation who wanted more than Billy Cotton and Perry Como. Pop music had arrived and the pirates broadcasting from the rough and tumble of the North Sea were so exciting. We had never heard the like before.

For me, the big difference was that you could really tell the presenters enjoyed the pop music they were playing as much as the young listeners. We thought we were cool cats, but they really were. Every time my mum tutted when I had Caroline on, I just turned the volume up.

When it first started broadcasting, I remember we were listening to it at my boarding school, Earsham Hall, Norfolk, when a teacher disturbed by 'rubbish' music stormed in. When he heard the DJ announce it was Radio Caroline, he turned pink with rage, picked up the radio and threw it on the floor, smashing it to pieces.

'RUBBISH,' he shouted again and stormed out. I don't think he was a fan of Mr Presley or those young upstarts, The Beatles.

I laughed, especially as it wasn't my radio!

Colin Nichol, DJ with Radios Atlanta, Caroline South, England and Britain, BBC Radios 1 and 2, British Forces Broadcasting Service:

I was a radio presenter in Australia before coming to the United Kingdom and had been working with pop stars like Cliff Richard. Bobby Rydell, Pat Boone and the Everly Brothers. I wanted to broaden my radio experience, so planned on coming to Britain.

I think England was swinging slightly when I arrived from Australia in April 1963, and The Beatles influence was already

most evident. However, it was early days, the feeling was confined mainly to pubs and clubs, and the mood of much of the country was still often sombre and almost post-war. Therefore, I'd say the pirate stations gave the movements of the era impetus and fuelled them. Suddenly, music was everywhere. Yes, it would have happened, but not as dramatically or as quickly, the timing was extraordinary, albeit by coincidence. So many things occurred around that time that contributed to a feeling of resurgence in Britain. What would have happened if Allan Crawford had got his project Radio Atlanta off the ground a year or two earlier, as almost happened? That's an interesting thought, I feel.

I have often been asked if we were politically 'aware' of the bigger picture, and if any of the comments on-air brought a change to laws introduced by the government of the day. I feel the political implications were the obvious ones, rather than as an undercurrent changing morality and attitudes. In that respect, it seems to me the pirates were not instigating but were reflecting and possibly magnifying developing movements. By obvious political implications, I refer to the legal and political interplay, which was at the level of the instigators of offshore radio and government, not at the level of the DJs or of what went on aboard ship. We tried to avoid politics, while reflecting changing attitudes – an interplay between broadcaster and audience – a case of developing interactive media to a new level. In fact, the political, rather than sociological aspect of the pirates came to the fore only toward the end of the saga when Caroline did

Left: Colin Nichol in 1965.

become overtly political, also becoming involved in an election and thereby demonstrating how unwise it was to do so.

The offshore stations did help new artists, record companies and songwriters – many music artists who would not have had exposure without the radio ships. Then there was the music itself and the significant change in that – the case of the Rolling Stones is often quoted. The new and increased amount of music spread worldwide, and influenced as it went. Part of that was the startling boost to the music industry in every way – more publishers, managers, promoters, record companies etc. The industry increased, and so the economy benefited as a result.

While pirate radio itself may not have directly influenced all aspects of fashion, they did so via the music industry and those associated with it. While it is frequently remarked upon, it is worth noting as well that the sheer audacity of the rebellious attitude many attributed to the pirates that tapped the anti-establishment element in many and hinted at possible new freedoms.

Offshore broadcasters had an effect upon society in fashion and attitudes as well as in music, and this spread because of the worldwide impact of the pirate ships. In briefer form, I'd say they showed anything was possible, new horizons opened and that the old limitations no longer applied.

Bryan Vaughan, DJ, Radios Atlanta, Caroline South, Luxembourg and Scotland:

The heritage of offshore radio was that it successfully introduced commercial radio to the UK. There could not have been better timing. The UK music industry was just starting to shine in the early sixties, but the advent of pirate radio gave many new artists a very important outlet that had previously been restricted to the BBC and night-time Radio Luxembourg. There is no doubt that many performers owe their recording careers to the pirates. A creative and commercial UK music industry, intensive pirate radio airplay and the wonders of Carnaby Street fashions created a perfect storm in the mid- to late sixties and the world listened to all things British.

Graham 'Spider' Webb, Radio Caroline North and South, Radio 2 and radio stations in Australia:

Prior to my arrival in England, I had been breakfast presenter on Australian radio stations. I joined Radio Caroline South in May 1965 and then moved to the North ship. One programme I distinctly remember is when I presented a two-hours broadcast from the deck of the MV *Caroline* for the wedding of Mick Luvzit in September 1966.

Back on the South ship, I was programme controller for a while and then news director when we broadcast 'Caroline Newsbeat', bringing news to the nation.

My most memorable time with Caroline was when the *Mi Amigo* ran aground. Reference has been made to that event in Chapter 1, suffice for me to say I looked out of the porthole that January evening and saw a light, which I thought was another ship about to ram us, but it was a bloke on the beach with a flashlight trying to find out what we were doing on 'his' beach.

I was proud to have been a pirate DJ and part of the offshore era. I just wish I had been there for a longer period of time. We were the catalyst for the start of the British invasion of the pop

music world. Had it not been for the likes of Caroline, London and other stations who gave them their break would we ever have heard of The Who, Small Faces, Rolling Stones, Moody Blues or the Kinks? They were all spun on the radio ships turntables and enjoyed by millions of listeners.

Left: The MV *Galaxy*, home to Radio London from 1964–67.

Right: DJ Bryan Vaughan with French singer Marie Vincent during her visit to Radio Caroline South in 1965 to promote her record 'Chip Chip'. David Kindred remembers the visit: 'I recall the trip to the ship from Harwich on a reasonably calm day was uneventful, although the return trip was quite rough and Marie was very ill with seasickness, and looked much less glamourous after a two-hour tender ride back to Harwich.'

Graham Webb in the cramped news studio on the *Mi Amigo*.

ACKNOWLEDGEMENTS

The authors are grateful to all those who have played any part in the offshore history, be they managers, DJs, engineers, cooks or crew members. It was indeed a most exciting time for offshore radio. It is hard to believe that Radio Caroline celebrated its fiftieth anniversary at Easter 2014, and Radio London at Christmas 2014.

Particular thanks go to Hans Knot in Holland, Jon Myer and Chris Edwards in England for reading through the manuscript and giving constructive advice.

To Johnny Beerling, former head of Radio 1 who has written the foreword, and to Peter Moore for his comments about Ronan O'Rahilly on the preface page and further on in the book about Radio Caroline today.

Interviews have taken place over many years with radio personalities and those who run websites who have given special quotes for the book, including Barbara Apostolides, Andy Archer, John Aston, Philip Birch, Tony Blackburn, David Clayton, Tom Edwards, Alex Hendricks, Derek James, Johnny Lewis, François Lhote, Gordon Mac, Colin Nichol, Mary and Chris Payne, Ronan O'Rahilly, Norman St John, Ed Stewart, Shaun Tilley, Alan 'Neddy' Turner, Bryan Vaughan, Johnnie Walker, and Graham Webb.

The internet has been used to check various facts, especially about the ships used for offshore radio. They include Wikipedia; Shipboard Radio Stations (Dr Adrian Peterson); broadcasting-fleet.com; Offshore Radio Fleet, marine broacasters.com; *Offshore Echos*; Offshore Radio Museum and Pirate Radio Hall of Fame.

Special thanks to Emily Tinker and the staff of Amberley Books for their enthusiasm and help during 2014.

A bibliography appears at the end of this book. Many books and magazines have been consulted and credited in the text. Apologies if there have been any omissions.

BIBLIOGRAPHY

Since Keith Skues wrote the original manuscript for *Pop Went the Pirates* in 1968, a number of books and magazines have been published about the offshore era that are well worth a read. The author consulted all these books and magazines while writing the text for *Pirate Radio: An Illustrated History* and is grateful to the publishers for allowing extracts to be used.

Barrett, Simon, *SOS, 10 Days in the Life of a Lady* (Music Radio Promotions, 1976).

Bishop, Gerry, *Offshore Radio* (Iceni Enterprises, 1975).

Burch, John A., *Wheel Turned Full Circle* (Caroline Movement, Grays, Essex, 1993).

Chapman, Robert, *Selling the Sixties* (Routledge, 1992).

Clark, Ray, *Radio Caroline: The True Story of the Boat That Rocked* (History Press, 2014).

Donovan, Paul, *The Radio Companion* (HarperCollins, 1991).

Elliot, Chris, *The Wonderful Radio London Story* (East Anglian Productions).

Harris, Paul, *Broadcasting From the High Seas* (Paul Harris Publishing, 1977).

Jackson, Jay, *The Pirates Who Waived the Rules* (Now Radio Communications, 1985).

Knot, Hans, *25 Years Radio Caroline Memories* (Benfleet, 1989).

Leonard, Mike, *From International Waters* (Forest Press, 1996).

Lodge, Tom, *The Ship That Rocked the World* (Bartley Press, 2010).

Monitor Magazine, Benfleet, Essex, 1972–1990.

Moore, Peter, *Butterfly Upon the Wheel* (*Offshore Echos* magazine, London, 1992).

Noakes, Bob, *Last of the Pirates* (Paul Harris Publishing, 1984).

Offshore Echos, 1986–2014.

Radio Magazine, 1992–2014.

Rusling, Paul, *The Lid Off Laser* (Pirate Publications, 1984).

Skues, Keith, *Radio Onederland: The Story of Radio One* (Landmark Press, 1968 [now Terence Dalton Ltd]).

Walker, Johnnie, *Johnnie Walker: The Autobiography* (Michael Joseph, 2007).

Websites About Offshore Radio

Offshore Radio Guide www.offshore-radio.de
      The ultimate resource, with news, pictures, audio, links to
      YouTube videos on offshore radio, and more.
Offshore Echos www.offshoreechos.com
      Publishers of *Offshore Echos*, the world's only magazine
      solely devoted to offshore radio. Comprehensive website
      with history, and CDs and DVDs about offshore radio.
Hans Knot www.hansknot.com
      Dutch media historian, author and writer of monthly
      International Radio Report.
Pirate Radio Hall of Fame www.offshoreradio.co.uk
      The DJs that worked on the offshore stations from the
      1960s, '70s and '80s
Radio London www.radiolondon.co.uk
      Devoted to all things Big L – Radio London from the 1960s.
Radio Review www.radioreview.org.uk
      Publishers of *Radio Review* magazine, UK and world
      radio news and features.
Radio Caroline www.radiocaroline.co.uk
      The home of internet broadcaster Radio Caroline.

Right: 5 November 1985 saw the Laser 558 radio ship *Communicator*
escorted into Harwich Harbour by the *Guardline Tracker* (*rear*). The
Guardline Tracker had been used by the Department of Trade and Industry
to blockade both Radio Caroline and Laser 558 since August that year. Laser
gave up the fight after technical problems and a lack of funds. The *Guardline
Tracker* was the sister ship the the *Communicator*, which was originally
named *Guardline Seeker*. Both ships had belonged to the Guardline Surveys
Ltd of Great Yarmouth.

INDEX

Tune

Volume

Ahern, Mike 34
Alexander, Paul 77
Allan, Tony 70, 74
Allen, Brian 92
Allen, Don 33, 71
Allen, Mike 33
Amsterdam 19, 35, 67, 68, 78, 101, 108, 111, 113, 123, 127, 135, 138, 139, 144
Anderson, Ray 101, 120, 139
Anderson, Tom 85, 91, 92, 107
Angela 71, 125
Animals, The 8, 11, 32
Archer, Andy 69, 77, 81, 82, 86, 143, 151
Arnold, P. P. 49
Arran, Lord and Lady 50
Australia 19, 30, 33, 35, 46, 74, 145, 147
Bacharach, Burt 32
Baeker, Captain George 112

Baldwin, Geoff 136, 137
Baltic 5, 17, 35, 36, 112, 126
Banks, Robin 71
Barrett, Simon 74, 77, 152
BBC 4, 6–9, 11, 20, 22, 23, 26, 29, 32, 35, 46, 50, 51, 54, 55, 83, 92, 94, 104, 108, 134, 140, 141, 143, 145, 147
BBC Northern Dance Orchestra 11
Beatles, The 8, 9, 11, 29, 32, 64, 145
Beerling, Johnny 7, 151
Belgium 17, 73, 100, 122, 138, 144
Benghazi 71
Bennett, Tony 57
Benson, Barry 49
Bentwaters, Suffolk 26
Berry, Colin 143
Berry, Dave 54
Bevins, Reginald 20

Birch, Philip 45, 53, 54, 56, 151
Bishop, Gerry 51, 152
Blackburn, Tony 6, 20, 33, 33–36, 39, 140, 142, 151
Blair, Chuck 51, 55
Blyth, Northumberland 129
Bolland, Fred 101
Bollier, Edwin 69, 70, 71, 123
Bon Jour 126
Bonney, Graham 29
Boone, Pat 145
Boonstra, Jelle 138
Brady, Pete 26, 45
Brentwood 45
Bridlington 129
Britain Radio 54, 57, 129, 131
British Forces Network 6, 23
Burch, John 138, 152

Byrds, The 26, 29

Calvert, Dorothy 59

Calvert, Reginald 26, 59, 61

Cameron, David 136

Cameron, Samantha 136

Canada 36

Capital Radio 78, 122, 123, 131

Chelmsford 45, 59

Chelsea 5, 18

Christian, Neil 51, 54

Chicago, Peter 74, 77, 78, 86

Clacton-on-Sea 19, 20, 26, 105, 122, 125, 133

Clark Dave 29, 54

Clark, Petula 32

Clark, Ray 143, 152

Clayton, David 141, 151

CNBC 13

Cogan, Alma 54

Colchester 45, 62

Como, Perry 145

Conniff, Ray 57

Copenhagen 114

Cordell, Denny 51

Cotton, Billy 145

Crawford, Allan 13, 14, 17, 112, 126, 146

Currie, Tony 139

D'Abo, Mike 29

Dale, Robbie 29, 34, 64, 128, 144, 145

Dallas, Texas 46

Dallon, Miki 50

Danger Man 61

Darrell, Guy 29, 49

Davis, Spencer 49

Day, Roger 77, 125, 145

de Zwart, Werner 77, 78

Dee, Simon 14, 18–20, 22, 32, 69, 73

Delfshaven 74, 123

Dencker, Theo 135

Denmark 110, 112, 126

Department of Trade and Industry 94, 98, 100, 154

Dioptric Surveyor 94

Dom, Baudouin 135

Draayer, Joost den 138

Du Crow, Peter 18

Dylan, Bob 29

East Anglian Productions 95, 100, 119, 152

East, Mick 81, 82

Edwards, Chris 135, 151

Edwards, Tom 143, 151

England, Steve 77

Eurosiege 118

Eve, Captain Martin 85, 133

Everly Brothers 145

Everett, Kenny 51

Faith, Adam 29

Faith, Percy 57

Faithfull, Marianne 49

Fame, Georgie 4

Farlowe, Chris 54

Felixstowe 5, 7–9, 11, 17, 18, 36, 53, 56, 58, 62, 64, 112, 119, 122, 126

Finland 17

Firth of Clyde 118

Fisher, Captain Willie 118

Fletcher, Bob 13

Fordyce, Keith 13

Forrester, Lt Cdr R.R. 121

France 17, 26, 74, 105, 125

France Radio Club 135, 136

Freeman, Alan 12, 32

Freewave Media Magazine 138

Frinton-on-Sea 46, 50, 67, 77, 114, 126, 130, 139

Gale, Roger 33

Galverston, Texas 121, 126

Gambia 117

Gardline Seeker 118

Gardline Tracker 94, 98

Garrick, David 29, 49

GBOK 14

Gerbers, Karel 135

Germany 23, 110, 111, 114, 118, 126, 132, 138

Gipps, Captain Martin 36

Golden Gate Strings 29

Gorleston 141

Grant, Julie 29

Great Yarmouth 141, 153

Greenore, Ireland 5, 13, 112, 113, 126

Groningen 110, 122, 131, 134, 138, 139

Hague, The 70, 71, 110

Hampshire, Keith 34

Hampshire, Susan 29

Hengeveld, Captain 18, 112

Hargreaves, Patrick 117

Harris, Nigel 88, 92

Harris, Paul 74, 152

Harris, Richard 16

Harris, Rick 97, 98, 100

Harwich 9, 20, 23, 26, 36, 42, 45, 49, 95, 98, 100, 101, 114, 116, 117, 119, 121, 148, 153

Hawkins, Dave 51

Heath, Edward 69

Healy, Ben 118

Hendricks, Alex 114, 151

Herman's Hermits 54

Holland/Netherlands 13, 17, 23, 36, 42, 44, 46, 64, 68–71, 74, 77–79, 100, 103, 100–113, 117, 122, 123, 125, 125, 129, 131, 132, 134, 137, 138, 151

Holland-on-Sea 9, 37, 39, 40, 69, 126, 139

Hollingdale, Paul 13

House of Commons 8, 20, 61, 64

Ifield, Frank 49

IJmuiden, Holland 35, 78, 121

Ilford 45

Independent Local Radio 6, 83, 94, 104, 137

Ipswich 7–9, 64, 73, 82

Isle of Man 12, 17, 18, 25, 64, 67, 112, 113, 126

Italy 30, 71, 125

ITV (Anglia) 46

Jackson, Jay 77, 92, 137, 152

Jackson-Hunter, John 78

Jacobs, David 13

James, Derek 145, 151

Jenkins, Hugh 61

Johnstone, Jack 118

Jones, Tom 32, 54, 141

Jurgens, Norbert 70

Katwijk aan Zee 64, 79, 111, 122

Kaye, Paul 45, 46

Kayne, Martin 58, 70

Keen, Alan 53

Kemp, Garry 33

Kennedy, Caroline 14

Kennedy, John F. 14

Kent, Roger 71

Kenya 6, 23

Kerr, Doug 18, 20, 22, 33

Kindred, David 7–10, 42, 53, 148

KING Radio 59, 60, 62

Kinks 8, 11, 148

Kiss FM 104

KLIF Radio 46

Klokkers, Captain Peter 30

Knock John Fort 61, 62

Knot, Hans 131, 134, 135, 138, 139, 151–153

Lady Kent 26

Laine, Denny 29

Landschoot, Adriaan van 73, 122

Laser 558 94, 95, 97, 100, 103, 107, 118, 119, 121, 136, 153

Laser 730 118, 119, 121

Laser Hot Hits 98, 100, 101, 118, 121

Lee, Peggy 57

Leighton, Jerry 181

Lennon, John 54, 83

Lennox, Mike 51

Lester, Ken 129

Lewis, Johnny 77, 107, 108, 151

Lewis, Jerry Lee 145

Lhote, Francois 135, 151

Libya 71, 73, 125

Liechtenstein 123, 133

Liverpool 78

Lloyd, Mike 77, 78

Lodge, Tom 18, 24, 29, 30, 34, 35, 39, 43, 48, 128, 152

Long Sandbank 81, 129

Los Bravos 29

Luvzit, Mick 36, 147

Maassluis 110

Mac, Gordon 104, 151

Magniez, Robert 135

Mann, Manfred 29

Manningtree   45, 121

Marine Broadcast (Offences) Bill   10, 57, 61, 64

Marine Offences Act   59, 64, 69, 77, 103, 112, 122, 126, 127, 129, 134, 144

Marseilles   132

Martin, Dean   57

Martin, Keith   18, 20

Mathis, Johnny   57

May, Paul   98

McGoohan, Patrick   61

McKenzie, Brian   71

Meister, Erwin   69, 70, 71, 123

Merike, Stevie   70

Ministry of Posts and Telecommuciations   69

Monitor Magazine   71, 135, 151

Moody Blues   29, 54, 148

Moore, Christopher   14

Moore, Peter   5, 105, 138, 151, 152

Moss, Don   13

Moss, Johnny   118

Mourkens, Mike   101

'Mr Tambourine Man'   26, 29

Muldoon, Spangles   77

Murphy, Judy aka Jodie Scott   92

Murray Mitch   29

Murray, Pete   13

Musicians' Union   11

MV *Aegir II*   79, 110, 111, 129

MV *Borkum Riff*   13, 64, 79, 111

MV *Caroline/Fredericia*   5, 17–19, 25, 36, 67, 73, 112, 113, 123, 125, 126, 147

MV *Cheeta II*   35, 36, 40, 42, 114–117

MV *Cito*   74, 131

MV *Comet*   59, 117, 118, 123

MV *Communicator*   9, 94, 95, 97, 98, 100, 101, 118–121, 153

MV *Galaxy*   9, 46–47, 49–53, 56, 119, 121, 122, 148

MV *Jeanine*   122, 123

MV *King David*   78, 122, 123, 131

MV *Magda Maria*   13

MV *Magdalena*   74, 123, 135

MV *Mebo II*   69–71, 73, 86, 123–125, 145

MV *Mi Amigo*   2, 9, 12, 15–26, 29, 30, 33–37, 39, 40, 42–44, 48, 67, 73, 74, 76, 77, 79, 80–82, 86, 91, 107, 112–114, 122, 123, 126–129, 134, 135, 141, 144, 145, 147, 150

MV *Norderney*   64, 79, 111

MV *Oceaan 7*   57, 129

MV *Offshore 1*   21–23, 26, 40, 42, 49, 56

MV *Olga Patricia/Laissez-Faire*   54, 57, 129–131

MV *Peace*   74, 131, 132

MV *Ross Revenge*   5, 9, 10, 74, 81–83, 85, 86, 88, 91, 92, 94, 101, 102, 104, 105, 107, 108, 121, 132, 133, 136, 137, 160

MV *Zeevaart*   122, 131

Nathan, Abie   131, 132

New Vaudeville Band   51

New York   32, 33, 118, 129, 132

New Zealand   74,

Newton, Martin   46

Nichol, Colin   17, 35, 40, 42, 114, 115, 145, 146, 151

Noakes, Bob   71, 139, 152

Noble, Paul   33, 34

Noordwijk   78, 123

Norway   17, 35, 69, 123 ,157

Norwich   51, 142

O'Rahilly, Ronan   4, 7, 13, 14, 18, 32, 35, 39, 40, 42–44, 46, 69, 73, 74, 77, 94, 101, 112, 114, 115, 151

O'Sullivan, Gibert   70

Ofcom   104, 108

Okinawa   121

Olthof, Rob   139

Out, Rob   79

Ouwerkerk, Holland   74, 113, 118, 122

Panama   36, 112, 118, 121, 125, 133

Parkeston Quay, Harwich   20, 121

Pearl Harbour   121

Pearson, 'Buster' Roland C.   135

Phonographic Performance Ltd   54

Pier Vick Ltd   54

Pierson, Don   46, 121

Pirate Radio News   137–139

Pitney, Gene   49

Platz, David   51

Presley, Elvis 145
Price, Alan 54
Prince Richard of Gloucester 49
Procol Harum 51
Project Atlanta 14, 59, 112, 126, 145, 147
Queenborough 133
Radio 1 6, 7, 9, 54, 55, 74, 88, 151
Radio 2 147
Radio 199 73, 127
Radio 227 54, 131
Radio 270 57, 122, 129
Radio 355 57, 58, 131
Radio 390 60–62, 143
Radio 819 101, 133
Radio Antilles 33
Radio Atlanta 12, 13, 15–17, 20, 22, 112, 126, 145–147
Radio Atlantis 73, 74, 77, 122, 123, 135, 137
Radio Caroline 2, 4, 5, 7–12, 14, 17–23, 25–27, 29, 30, 32–36, 39, 40, 45, 46, 60, 61, 64, 37, –70, 73, 74, 76–79, 81–83, 85, 86, 88, 91, 92, 94, 95, 101, 103–105, 107, 108, 112–114, 122, 123, 126–129, 131–138, 140–148, 151–153, 160
Radio City 26, 30, 59, 60–62, 143, 144
Radio Condor 78, 122
Radio Delmare 79, 110, 111, 129, 135
Radio Dolfijn 54, 57, 131
Radio East Anglia 51, 53

Radio England 54, 55, 57, 64, 129, 131
Radio Essex 61, 62
Radio Invicta 59, 60, 62
Radio London 6, 9, 26, 34, 42, 45–47, 49–57, 114, 119, 121, 122, 129, 131, 140, 141, 143
Radio Luxembourg 4, 13, 23, 34, 46, 92, 145, 147
Radio Magazine 137
Radio Mercur 13, 35, 114
Radio Mi Amigo 73, 74, 76, 123, 127, 135
Radio Monique 100–102, 107, 133
Radio Nord 13, 14, 17, 22, 126
Radio Norfolk 141, 143
Radio Northsea International 9, 69, 70, 73, 86, 98, 103, 123–125
Radio Nova International 71, 125
Radio Review 136, 137, 153
Radio Scotland 3, 59, 94, 117, 118, 123, 147
Radio Seagull 73, 79, 127
Radio Sutch 59, 62
Radio Syd 14, 35, 114
Radio Veronica 13, 36, 64, 70, 71, 77, 79, 111, 118, 121, 135, 138, 140, 144
Ramsey Bay 12, 17, 18, 67, 112
Ramsgate 83
Red Sands 59–62
Reiner, Horst 125
Reynolds, Chuck aka Randall Lee Rose 92, 158

Richard, Cliff 45, 145
Richardson, Mark 29
Rochester 69, 133
Rochford 60, 61
Rogers, Dave 70
Rolling Stones 4, 8, 9, 11, 14, 147, 148
Romford 45
Rose, Howard C. (Crispian St John) 70, 137
Rosko, Emperor 24, 27, 29, 34, 48, 128
Rosyth 133
Rotterdam 71, 79, 110–112, 125
Rowe, Normie 49
Royal Navy 14, 62, 70, 112
Royal Engineers 61, 62
Ruffin, Jimmy 51
Saunders, George 30, 35, 39
Scadden, Bill 20, 39, 44
Scandinavia 13, 117
Scarborough 57, 59, 129
Scheveningen 13, 70, 73, 78, 80, 110, 111, 127, 129, 145
Scotland Yard, London 20
Sealand 61, 62, 119
Shaw, Sandie 54
Shields, Tommy 118
Shivering Sands 59, 60, 62, 143
Sinatra, Frank 57
Skues, Keith 6, 10, 30, 33, 53, 140, 143, 144
Slikkerveer, Netherlands 69, 71, 123, 125
Small Faces 54, 148

Smedley, Major Oliver 59

Smith, Jimmy 29

Southend-on-Sea 73, 77, 78, 82, 105, 127, 133

Springfield, Dusty 54, 158

St John, Norman 30, 34–36, 39, 56, 151

Stanley, Doug 13

Starling, Patrick 30, 35, 39, 43

Stevens, Sir Jocelyn 17

Stewart, Ed 51, 53, 151

Sunk Head Tower 61, 62

Sutch, Screaming Lord 59

Swainson, Richard 51

Swanson, Arnold 14

Sweden 13, 14, 17, 35, 110, 114, 126

Switzerland 71

Sydney, Australia 19, 33

Sydney, Jon 33

Tack, Sylvain 74, 135

Tampa 121

Taylor, Derek 29

Tel Aviv 132

Teret, Janet 36

Teret, Ray 36

Territorial Sea Act 81, 100, 121

Thames Estuary 9, 14, 59–62, 82, 127, 133

Thomson, Carl 35

Tilbury 105, 108, 133

Tilley, Shaun 83, 151

Times, The 18, 110

Titan 35, 126

Tollerfield, Russell 51

Tower Radio 61, 62

Travis, Dave Lee 35, 39, 47

Tremeloes 50

Trinity House 117, 125, 138

Troon 118

Turner, Alan 'Neddy' 18, 151

Turner, Ike and Tina 49

Twice as Much 49

Twinkle 29

United States of America 54, 74

USS Density 45, 46, 121

Utrecht 112, 113

Van de Marel 113, 118, 122, 123

van Dam, Gerard 135

van der, Captain Kamp 125

van der Linden, Captain Tom 127

van der Ven, Martin 139

Vaughan Bryan 18, 19, 23, 26, 33, 147, 148

Venturous 112

Verweij brothers 70, 111, 138

Viking Saga 26

Vincent, Marie 29, 148

Voice of Peace 74, 107, 131, 132, 137

Volans 70, 94

Wadner, Britt 14, 35, 40, 42, 114, 115

Walker Brothers 54

Walker, Johnnie 64, 144, 151, 152

Walker, Willy 55

Walton and Frinton Lifeboat 19, 20

Walton, Bob 33

Walton-on-the-Naze 9, 17, 26, 35, 39, 61, 122, 125, 159

Washington, Geno 49, 54

Webb, Graham 34, 35, 39, 147, 150, 151

Wedgwood Benn, Anthony 20

Weltens, Arno 138

Wendens Ambo 59

Wesley, Mark 69

Wehrmacht 126

West, Alan 69, 70, 139

West, Dave 139

West, Ian 51

Whitstable 60

Wijsmuller Salvage Company 67, 68, 73, 112, 123

Willemsen, Steph 122

Wilson, Harold 4, 69, 70

Wireless Telegraphy Act 61, 103, 104

Windsor (Withers), Tony 18, 51, 58

Winn, Lt John C. Jnr 26

Woodbridge 82

World Mission Radio 133

Wrury, Captain Willy 35

YouTube 144, 153

Zaandam, Holland 35, 42, 111, 122, 126

Zandvoort, Holland 78

ABOUT THE AUTHORS

The Radio Caroline ship *Ross Revenge* was moved to the River Blackwater, near to Bradwell, Essex, on 31 July 2014, after spending ten years at Tilbury Docks. This photograph was taken as the ship moved out into the River Thames at Tilbury, escorted by two tugs. (*Photograph by Chris Dunford*)

KEITH SKUES was a pirate disc jockey on Radio Carolina and Radio London. He has also worked for Radio Luxembourg, was one of the original presenters for BBC Radio One, programme director for Radio Hallam, and can still be heard on BBC local radio for the eastern counties. He was appointed MBE in 2004 for his contribution to radio.

DAVID KINDRED has worked in professional photography for over fifty years. He was a staff photographer for the *East Anglian Daily Times* and *Evening Star* when he took these unique and beautiful photos of the pirate radio stations and their crew.